Guiding Your Friends Around
Shinjuku Ni-chome in English

英語で新宿二丁目を紹介する本

森村明生●著
ポール・ネルム●訳
松沢呉一●監修

ポット出版

Contents

目次

8 **S**hinjuku Ni-chome MAP
新宿駅周辺
新宿二丁目

14 **H**istory of Shinjuku Ni-chome **1**
From a red-light district to one of the world's biggest gay towns
色街から、世界最大級の
ゲイ・タウンへ

16 **H**istory of Shinjuku Ni-chome **2**
Ever diversifying, Ni-chome is a place for gays to meet
多様化する、ゲイたちの
「出会いの場」

18 **H**istory of Shinjuku Ni-chome **3**
Tokyo Pride Parade and the Tokyo Rainbow Festival
東京プライドパレードと
東京レインボー祭り

20 **P**rologue
You could say he's like Brad Pitt in his younger days.
若い頃のブラッド・ピットに
似てるかも

22 **T**he Characters in This Book
この本に登場する人たち

25 **S**cene **1**
Off to Shinjuku
いざ、新宿へ

26 **D**ialog **1**
Masashi, you're holding on to his hand too much.
まさしさん、手を握りすぎですよ

28 **D**ialog **2**
Actually, it's Japanese guys I like.
実は日本の男の子が好きなんです

30 **D**ialog **3**
When did you come out?
カミングアウトはいつ？

32 **D**ialog **4**
What's a "o-bon" vacation?
お盆休み？

34 **D**ialog **5**
Hey, there's an "o-nakama"!
あら、お仲間さん発見！

36 **D**ialog **6**
How about a Japanese "izakaya" pub?
居酒屋なんてどうかしら？

38 **D**ialog **7**
It's fun, like being in a hide-out.
隠れ家みたいで楽しいですね

40 **D**ialog **8**
"Niku-jaga" is the best weapon to catch a guy.
肉じゃがは、男を落とす最強兵器よ

42 **D**ialog **9**
Can women go inside gay bars?
ゲイバーって女性も入れるの？

44 **D**ialog **10**
That's where people who like to cross-dress get together.
ここは、女装をしたい人が集まるお店よ

47 **Scene 2**

Everything is a first for me.
何もかもが、初体験

48 **D**ialog **1**
The sign "Members only" indicates a gay bar!?
「会員制」はゲイバーの目印！？

50 **D**ialog **2**
Mark, you're gay, too, right?
マークさんもゲイなんですよね？

52 **D**ialog **3**
So, we'll have four "chuhai" mixed with Oolong tea.
じゃあ、ウーロン茶割りを4つで

54 **D**ialog **4**
Here are your "o-toshi."
はい、お通しよ

56 **D**ialog **5**
Someone has started singing karaoke.
カラオケが始まりましたね

58 **D**ialog **6**
Your first crush was a "deli-hel boy"!?
デリヘルボーイが、初恋の子！？

60 **D**ialog **7**
I think he was probably gay, too.
彼もたぶんゲイだったと思うんですよ

62 **D**ialog **8**
After he finishes distributing condoms....
コンドームを配り終えたら……

64 **D**ialog **9**
Are they all gay?
あれはみんなゲイなのかな？

66 **D**ialog **10**
I hear there's about 200 to 300 gay-related places.
200〜300軒はゲイ関係のお店らしいよ

69 **S**cene **3**

All sorts of gay bars, all sorts of gays
ゲイバーいろいろ、
ゲイもいろいろ

70 **D**ialog **1**
Can a woman go in there by herself?
女の子だけで来てもいいのかしら？

72 **D**ialog **2**
Is the clientele at each gay bar completely different?
ゲイバーによって、客層は全然違うの？

74 **D**ialog **3**
I'll wait outside, so you guys go on ahead.
メンオンリーだから外で待つわ

76 **D**ialog **4**
My friends call me a "rice queen."
僕は友達から「ライスクイーン」といわれています

78 **D**ialog **5**
Oh dear, here comes a pain in the neck!
あら、面倒くさい子が来たわ！

80 **D**ialog **6**
Sister Masako!?
まさ子ネエさん!？

82 **D**ialog **7**
What's an "SG-kei"?
SG系って何？

84 **D**ialog **8**
Japanese gays are lenient toward fat guys.
日本のゲイは、脂肪に寛容なんですね……

86 **D**ialog **9**
I've been constantly dumped the past few years.
アタシはここ何年も捨てられっぱなしよ

88 **D**ialog **10**
The buildings are left from the old red-light district days.
赤線時代の建物が今も残っているの

91 **Scene 4**
Ni-chome as an information center
二丁目の、情報ステーション

92 Dialog 1
This street is called "Lily Path."
「百合の小道」と呼ばれているの

94 Dialog 2
Here we are at "akta."
「akta」に到着

96 Dialog 3
That's the ultimate form of safe sex!
それは、究極のセーフセックスですね

98 Dialog 4
Don't treat it like somebody else's problem!
他人事みたいな顔しないのっ！

100 Dialog 5
That's what's known as a gay shop.
ここはいわゆるゲイショップよ

102 Dialog 6
They're smaller and thicker than American gay magazines.
アメリカのゲイ雑誌より小さくて厚いですね

104 Dialog 7
Look at how many gay DVDs there are!
ゲイDVD、ものすごくたくさんありますね

106 Dialog 8
There's an "O-né" celebrity!
おネエタレントを目撃！

108 Dialog 9
"Fujoshi" have become a hot topic of conversation.
「腐女子」も話題よ

110 Dialog 10
So it's sort of an information center for Ni-chome as well.
ここも、二丁目の情報センターなんですね

112 **Scene 5**
Various facts about Ni-chome you wanted to know
もっと知りたい、いろんな二丁目

114 Dialog 1
Ni-chome is really a scary place, so full of temptations!
二丁目は誘惑だらけの恐ろしい街……

116 Dialog 2
That toilet is a "hattenba."
そのトイレはハッテン場よ

118 Dialog 3
What do mean by "new half" and "onabe"?
ニューハーフとかおなべって、何ですか？

120 Dialog 4
What do gays think about straights who visit Ni-chome?
二丁目に来るノンケをどう思っているんですか？

122 Dialog 5
Well, if it isn't the "busu" one!
あら、ブス、いらっしゃい！

124 Dialog 6
Let's go to an "uri-sen" bar next!
じゃあ今度は、売り専のお店に行くわよ！

126 Dialog 7
This is the kind of place where it pays to have fun!
こういうところは楽しんだもんがちよ！

128 Dialog 8
Ryo is a "cho-ikemen."
リョウくんって超イケメン

130 Dialog 9
How about if we go to a "fundoshi" bar?
ふんどしバーもあるわよ

132 Dialog 10
Can foreigner go to "hattenba" in Ni-chome, too?
二丁目のハッテン場は外国人も入れるの？

Contents

134 **Scene 6**

Joining the Tokyo Pride Parade
東京プライドパレードを、歩く

136 **D**ialog **1**
Shall we go to Yoyogi Park now?
さあ、代々木公園に移動するわよ！

138 **D**ialog **2**
Which float shall we walk with?
どのフロートと一緒に歩く？

140 **D**ialog **3**
They're booths set up by the Parade's sponsors.
パレードのスポンサーによる出展ブースだよ

142 **D**ialog **4**
Always ready with a comeback, you fag!
口の減らないオカマね

144 **D**ialog **5**
The "Brass with Everybody!" event is about to start.
「"みんな"でブラス！」が始まるよ

146 **D**ialog **6**
The Parade is about to begin, finally!
さあ、いよいよパレード出発ね！

148 **D**ialog **7**
Somehow it really made me so happy.
何だかとっても幸せな気持ち

150 **D**ialog **8**
Are there any LGBT politicians in Japan who have come out?
カミングアウトした政治家はいるの？

152 **D**ialog **9**
Are they all volunteers?
彼らは全員、ボランティアなんですか？

154 **D**ialog **10**
We've been together the whole time since last night.
昨夜からずっと一緒だったね……

156 **Scene 7**

The only time Ni-chome has a festival each year!
年に一度の、祭りの夜

158 **D**ialog **1**
That's what we call an "o-mikoshi."
あれは御神輿というんだよ

160 **D**ialog **2**
There are sure a lot of food stalls here.
屋台もたくさん出ているのね

162 **D**ialog **3**
The Festival always closes with an "eisaa" dance.
お祭りの最後はエイサーで

164 **D**ialog **4**
Esmralda is going to do a show.
エスムラルダがショーをやるんですよ

166 **D**ialog **5**
They even hold a night for chubby chasers.
デブ専ナイトの日もあるんですね

168 **D**ialog **6**
Japanese drag queens are really something else!
日本のドラァグクイーンは面白いですね

170 **D**ialog **7**
Are there particular artists popular among gays in Japan?
ゲイに人気の芸能人たち

172 **D**ialog **8**
I have something important to say to Mark now.
僕、今からマークに大事な話があるんだ

174 **D**ialog **9**
I'd be happy to be your "aikata."
相方になってもらえたら嬉しい

176 **D**ialog **10**
Let's let the young couple be by themselves.
あとは若い二人に任せて……

46 **C**olumn **1**
ゴールデン街にもあるレズビアンやゲイの店
There are also lesbian and gay establishments in Shinjuku Golden-Gai.

68 **C**olumn **2**
二丁目にある3つのお寺
The three temples of Ni-chome

90 **C**olumn **3**
芸能人と二丁目
Celebrities and Ni-chome

112 **C**olumn **4**
ゲイブームと二丁目
The "gay boom" and Ni-chome

134 **C**olumn **5**
インターネットと二丁目
The Internet and Ni-chome

156 **C**olumn **6**
二丁目のさまざまなお店
Various kinds of establishments in Ni-chome

178 **E**pilogue
You two really are in love.
そして、二人は……

180 **I**ndex
索引

186 **I**nfomation
店情報

Shinjuku Ni-chome MAP

Shinjuku Station area | 新宿駅周辺

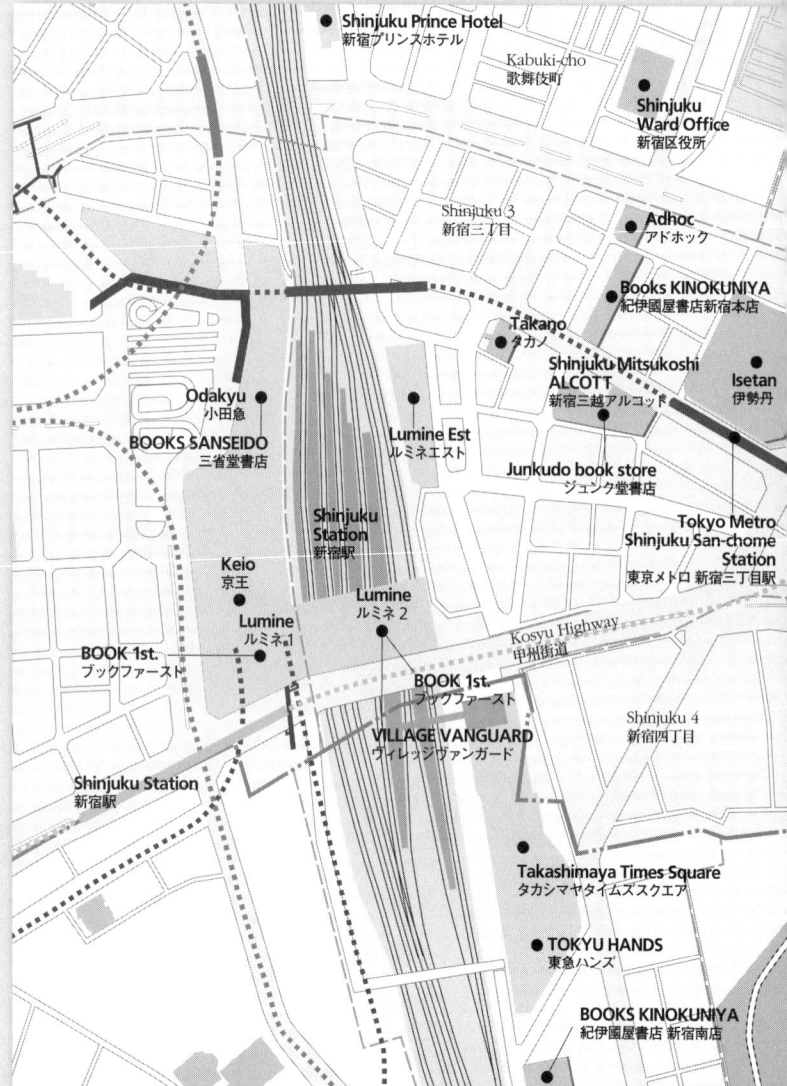

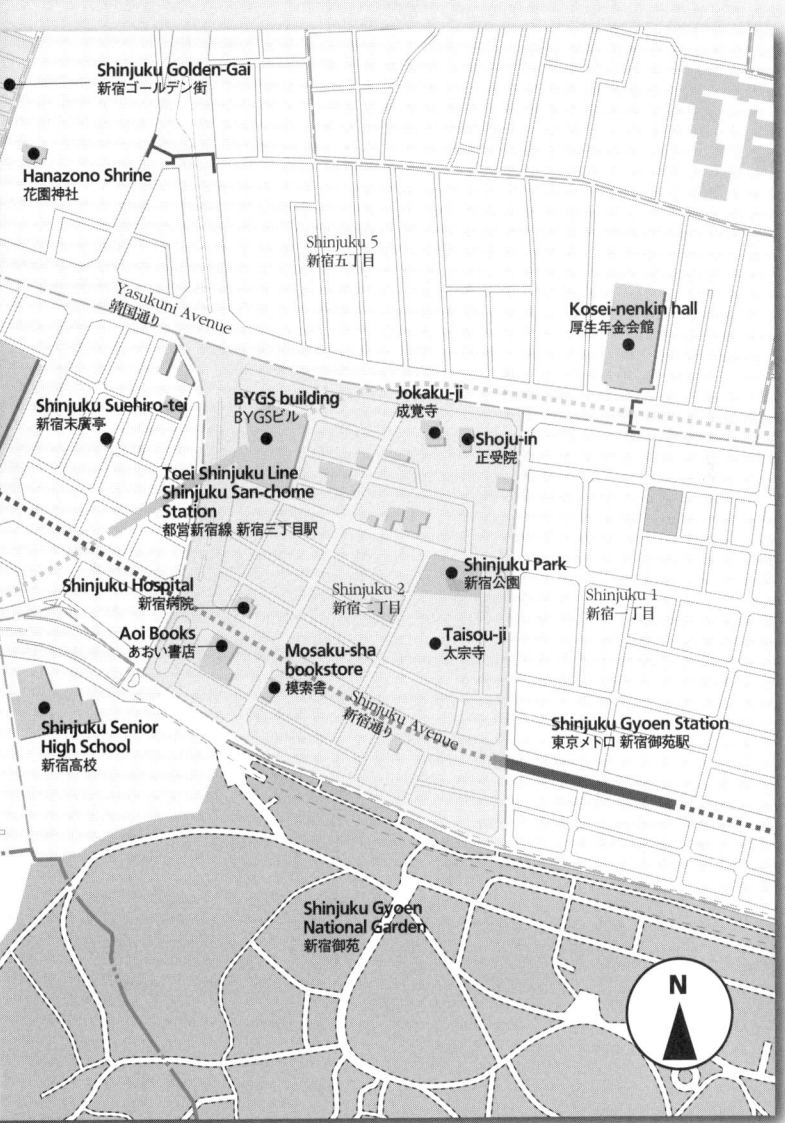

Shinjuku Ni-chome ｜ 新宿二丁目

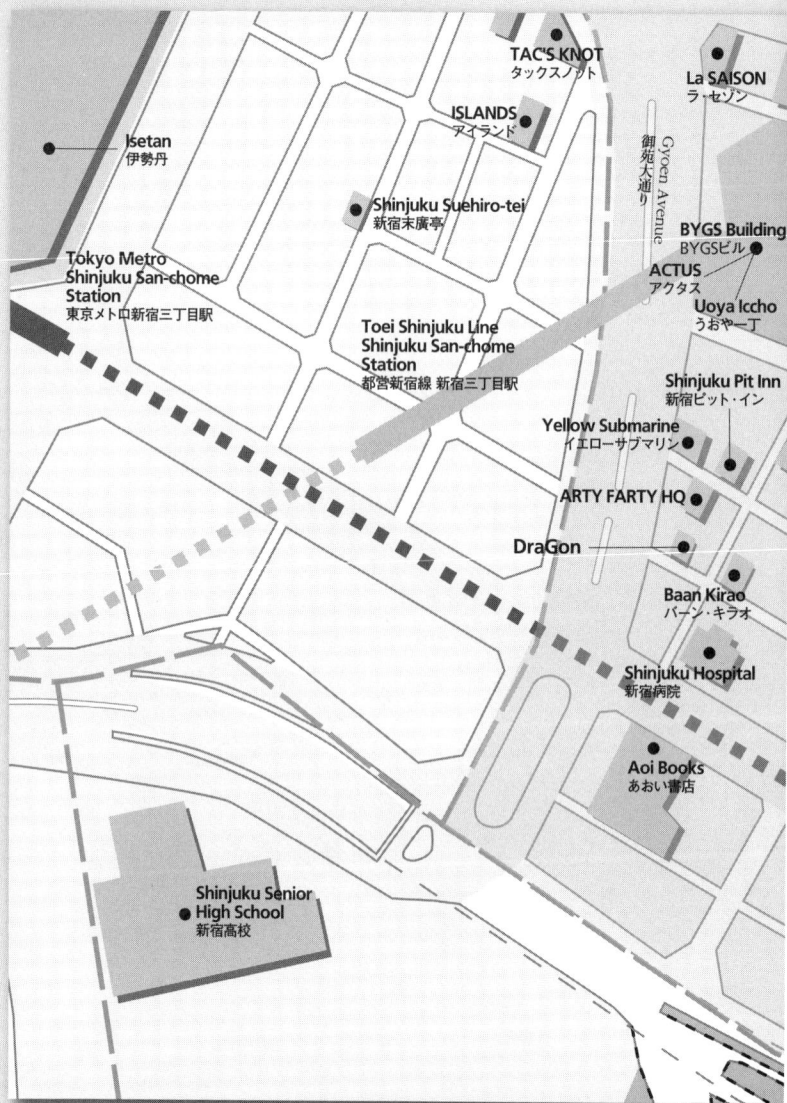

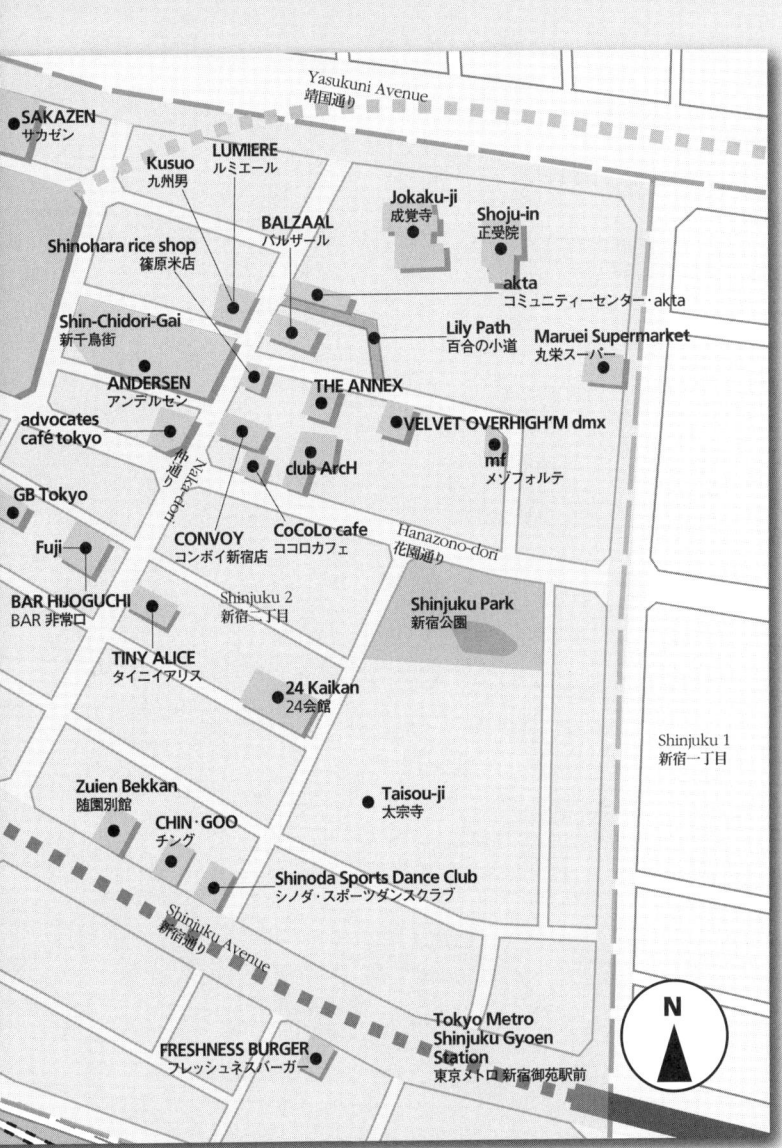

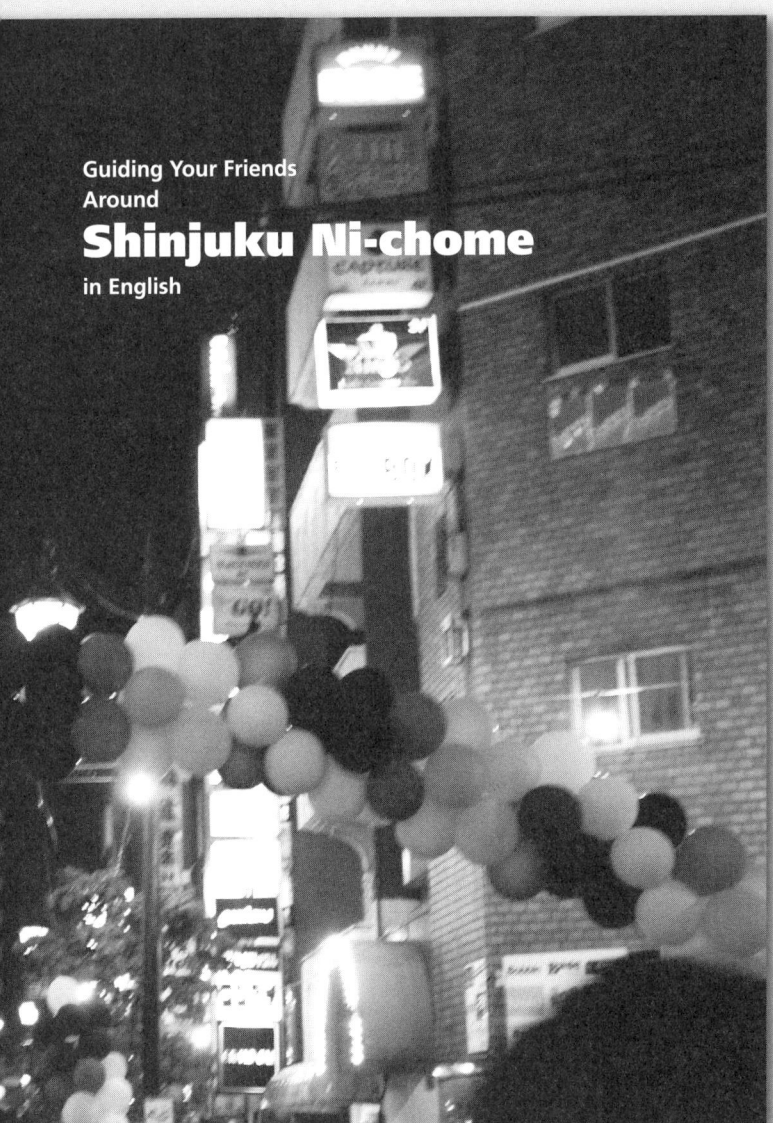

Guiding Your Friends Around
Shinjuku Ni-chome
in English

History of Shinjuku Ni-chome 1

From a red-light district to one of the world's biggest gay towns

Shinjuku Ni-chome is situated to the east of Shinjuku Station, bounded on the north by Yasukuni Avenue and on the south by Shinjuku Gyoen (National Garden).
In the early part of the Edo Era (1603-1868), in February 1699, a post station (i.e., lodgings area along a trunk road) called Naito Shinjuku (literally "Naito New Inn") was set up in the vicinity of the current Ni-chome in the old shogunate capital of Edo (now Tokyo). Working in the "hatagoya" (inns) and teahouses in the area were courtesans (i.e., prostitutes) called "meshimori-onna" (literally "meal-serving women," or women who took care of travelers at such inns, including their sexual needs), making Naito Shinjuku one of Edo's biggest red-light zones. In the Taisho Era (1912-26) and thereafter, this district was called Shinjuku Yukaku ("yukaku" meaning licensed quarter), flourishing with a clientele of educated intellectuals and salaried office workers. However, it was destroyed by bombing-related fires in 1945, and after the war, became an "aka-sen" area, or a red-light district. With the passing of the Anti-prostitution Act in 1958, however, the curtain closed on the area's history as a pleasure district.
The first appearance of gay bars in Ni-chome was in the 1960s, as they opened up in buildings abandoned by the former red-light establishments. By the early 1970s, then, the area had already taken on the shape of a gay-bar district. Nowadays, there are some 200 to 300 bars and clubs catering to homosexuals in the area, concentrated around Ni-chome's main street, Naka-dori. The area is featured often in the Japanese media, and is famous as one of the world's biggest gay towns.

色街から、
世界最大級のゲイ・タウンへ

　新宿二丁目は新宿駅の東側に位置し、北を靖国通り、南を新宿御苑に挟まれた街です。

　江戸時代初期（1699年2月）、このあたりに宿場（内藤新宿）が開設されました。宿場内の旅籠屋や茶屋には「飯盛女」と呼ばれる遊女が置かれ、内藤新宿は色街として栄えることに。大正時代以降は「新宿遊郭」と呼ばれ、インテリ層やサラリーマンを対象に全盛期を迎えましたが、1945年、戦災により焼失。終戦後は、「赤線地帯」と呼ばれる売春地域となり、1958年の「売春防止法」施行に伴い、「遊郭の街」としての歴史を終えました。

　二丁目にゲイバーができはじめたのは、1960年代以降。空き家となった元赤線の店などを利用して営業を始め、1970年前後にはすでに、ゲイバー街が形成されていたといわれています。現在では、メインストリートの仲通りを中心としたエリアに、200軒から300軒の、同性愛者向けのバーやクラブなどが集中。メディアに登場することも多く、世界最大級のゲイ・タウンとして知られています。

History of Shinjuku Ni-chome 2

Ever diversifying, Ni-chome is a place for gays to meet

Until just a dozen or so years ago, the only ways that Japanese gays could meet each other were in gay bars, through personal ads in gay magazines, and in cruising spots. However, ever since the late 1990s, the spread of the Internet and mobile (cell) phones has enabled the emergence of social networking services (SNSs) such as "mixi," which is the Japanese equivalent to "Myspace" or "Friendster," along with dating websites, exponentially expanding the breadth of encounters and exchanges gays can have with each other.

Since the early 1990s, moreover, there has been a so-called "gay boom" in Japan, centered on the media, as well as the influence of various gay liberation movements. More than before, there are a lot more people who accept their own gayness, as well as those who are actively open about it. In step with that, the level of activity by so-called "activity circles" among gays sharing the same interests——sports, music, hobbies, etc.——has also intensified. There has also been an increase in the number of gay bars opening up in other parts of Tokyo, such as Shibuya, Shimbashi, and Ueno. All of those social changes have combined to gradually change the nature of Ni-chome as a place for gays to get together and meet each other.

Meanwhile, in recent years, the number of heterosexuals frequenting Ni-chome alongside gays has grown as well, with more and more gay bars and club events allowing straight people in. Ni-chome can thus probably said to be entering a transitory stage, from a meeting place just for gays, to one where a lot of different people can get together.

多様化する、ゲイたちの「出会いの場」

　ほんの十数年前まで、日本のゲイたちの出会いの場は、ゲイバーや雑誌の文通欄、ハッテン場等に限られていました。しかし1990年代後半以降、インターネットや携帯電話の普及により、mixiをはじめとするSNS（ソーシャル・ネットワーキング・サービス）や出会い系サイトが登場し、ゲイたちの出会いや交流の幅は、飛躍的に拡大しています。

　また、1990年代前半にメディアを中心に発生したゲイ・ブームや、さまざまなゲイ・リベレーション活動の影響もあって、以前より、自分がゲイであることを受け入れ、かつオープンにできる人が多くなってきました。それに伴い、スポーツや音楽など、趣味を同じくするゲイたちのサークルも活発化しています。さらに、渋谷や新橋、上野などにオープンするゲイバーが増えており、こうした社会状況の変化が、ゲイたちの「出会いの場」としての二丁目のあり方を、徐々に変えつつあるといわれています。

　一方で、近年、二丁目でゲイと共に遊ぶ異性愛者が増え、異性愛者でも入ることのできるゲイバーやクラブイベントが、以前より多くなっているようです。今、二丁目は「ゲイだけの出会いの場」から「さまざまな人の出会いの場」への過渡期にあるといえるのかもしれません。

History of Shinjuku Ni-chome **3**

Tokyo Pride Parade and the Tokyo Rainbow Festival

The first Tokyo Lesbian & Gay Parade (TLGP) for LGBTs (lesbian, gay, bisexual, transgender, and other sexual minorities) was held in August 1994, hosted by the planning committee consisting mainly of ILGA Japan members, led by Teishiro Minami (1931-). Thereafter, the parade was held the following two years, in 1995 and 1996, but effectively went defunct over the next few years. It was succeeded in August 2000 by a parade organized by the planning committee run by Hideki Sunagawa (1967-). In 2005, Tokyo Pride was established as the parent organization running the TLGP, and the Tokyo Pride Parade has been held annually thereafter each August in Shibuya (Tokyo). The official name since 2007 is Tokyo Pride Parade.

Many bars and clubs in Ni-chome act as sponsors in support of the Tokyo Pride Parade, and have gotten together since 2005 to enter the Shinjuku Ni-chome Promotion Association float in that parade.

Also, since 2000, the Tokyo Rainbow Festival has been held every August or September, hosted by the same association. In years when the Tokyo Pride Parade is held, the Festival is either held on the same day or the next day. That event also enjoys huge crowds.

東京プライドパレードと東京レインボー祭り

　1994年8月、ILGA日本（代表・南定四郎(みなみていしろう)）を中心とした実行委員会による、日本における最初のLGBT（レズビアン、ゲイ、バイセクシュアル、トランスジェンダーなどのセクシュアルマイノリティ）のパレード「東京レズビアン・ゲイ・パレード」が開催されました。このパレードはその後1995年、1996年にも開催されましたが、数年後、実質的に消滅。かわって2000年8月、砂川秀樹を代表とする実行委員会が「東京レズビアン＆ゲイパレード」（TLGP）を開催。2005年に、TLGPを運営する母体として「東京プライド」が設立され、以後毎年8月に、東京・渋谷で、「東京プライドパレード」（2007年より名称変更）が実施されています。

　二丁目のバーやクラブなどの多くが、スポンサーとして、この東京プライドパレードを支えており、2005年からは「新宿二丁目振興会フロート」も出展しています。

　一方、2000年から毎年8月または9月に、新宿二丁目振興会主催による「東京レインボー祭り」が行われており（パレード開催年には、パレードの当日または翌日に開催）、こちらも大きな賑わいを見せています。

Prologue

You could say he's like Brad Pitt in his younger days.

Daisuke: Masashi, thanks for coming despite the heat. This is my friend from college days, Miho.

Miho: Daisuke always talks a lot about you.

Masashi: Hmm, I wonder what it is he says. Anyway, you said you wanted to ask me something?

Daisuke: Well, you see … next weekend, we'd like you to show us around Shinjuku Ni-chome.

Masashi: If you're gonna go prowling around Ni-chome, go do it yourself! Don't try to take advantage of me!

Daisuke: Actually, it's not me whom I want you to show around.

Miho: When I was studying overseas at a university in New York, I made friends with a gay guy named Mark, and he's coming to Japan next week to take part in the Tokyo Pride Parade.

Masashi: Hmm, I see. So, then what?

Daisuke: Mark wants to visit Ni-chome, and I thought it would be the best bet to ask an expert on Ni-chome like you, Masashi, to do the honor.

Masashi: No way, no way! I'm real busy now getting ready for the parade. Just for my information, though, what kind of guy is this Mark?

Miho: Maybe you could say he's like Brad Pitt in his younger days.

Masashi: Why didn't you say that earlier? Now I feel more like doing it.

Daisuke: But didn't you just say you were busy?

Masashi: I can solve that situation somehow!

若い頃のブラッド・ピットに似てるかも

8月はじめの日曜日の夜。喫茶店で、何やら話している大輔と美穂。
そこへまさしが登場。2人はまさしに、ある頼みごとをする。

大輔：まさしさん、暑い中すみません。こちらは、僕の大学時代の友達の美穂です。

美穂：いつも大輔くんから、お噂はうかがってます。

まさし：一体どんな噂だか。で、相談って何？

大輔：実は……。来週末、まさしさんに、新宿二丁目を案内していただきたいんです。

まさし：二丁目の開拓ぐらい、自力で頑張りな！甘えんじゃないよ！

大輔：いや、案内してほしいのは、僕じゃないんです。

美穂：私、大学時代にニューヨークの大学に留学したことがあって。その時に仲良くなったマークというゲイの男の子が、来週、東京のパレードに参加するために、日本に遊びに来るんです。

まさし：ふーん。それで？

大輔：マークが二丁目にも行きたがっているので、二丁目通のまさしさんに案内してもらうのが確実だと思って。

まさし：だめよ、だめ。アタシ、パレードの準備で忙しいの。……ちなみにマークって、どんな男なの？

美穂：若い頃のブラッド・ピットに似てるかも……。

まさし：それを早く言ってよ！　やる気出てきた。

大輔：でも、今忙しいんじゃ……。

まさし：そんなもん、何とかするわよ！

The Characters in This Book

マーク (24歳)　Mark (24)
ボストンで生まれ、現在ニューヨークの大学院に通っているアメリカ人のゲイ。
日本人の男の子が好き。
A gay American, born in Boston,
and now going to graduate school in New York.
Has a preference for Japanese guys.

大輔 (24歳)　Daisuke (24)
電機メーカーにつとめるサラリーマンで、ゲイ。
英会話教室に通っていたことがあり、英語も少し話せる。
A worker at an electronics manufacturer who happens to be gay.
Thanks to attending English conversation classes,
he can speak the language somewhat.

美穂 (23歳)　Miho (23)
大学院生で、大輔の大学時代の友人。ニューヨークに留学したことがあり、その時にマークと知り合った。
Now a graduate student, has been a friend of Daisuke's from college days.
Previously studied abroad in New York, where she got to know Mark.

まさし (35歳)　Masashi (35)
フリーのデザイナー。大輔のゲイ友だちで、二丁目通。
口は悪いが面倒見はいい、典型的なおネエさんタイプ。
A freelance designer and a gay friend of Daisuke's.
An expert on Ni-chome. Has a wicked tongue, but takes care of his friends well.
A typical queenie gay.

この本に登場する人たち

健一(24歳) **Ken'ichi** (24)
デリヘルボーイ
Deli-hel boy

太郎(26歳) **Taro** (26)
外専ゲイ
A gay Japanese man who has a preference for Westerners.

レイコ(?歳) **Reiko** (?)
ニューハーフショーパブ「ラ・セゾン」のショーガール
"Show girl" at the "new half" show pub bar " La SAISON"

リョウ(21歳) **Ryo** (21)
売り専の店「アンデルセン」のボーイ
Money boy working at the "ANDERSEN" money-boy bar

たけし(33歳) **Takeshi** (33)
まさしのおネエ友達
Masashi's queenie gay friend

スズキヨウヘイ(24歳) **Yohei Suzuki** (24)
マークの初恋の相手
Mark's first crush, when he was in grade school

Scene 1

Off to Shinjuku

いざ、新宿へ

Dialog 1

Masashi, you're holding on to his hand too much.

Miho: Hi!

Daisuke: Hi there. Masashi, you seem all revved up.

Masashi: Mind your own business! Hi, Miho! Oh, is this Mark?

Miho: Yes. Mark, this is a friend of mine from college, Daisuke. And standing next to him is Masashi, who will be showing us around Shinjuku Ni-chome later.

Mark: It's a pleasure to meet you.

Daisuke: Nice to meet you, too, I'm Daisuke.

Masashi: I'm Masashi. It's a pleasure to meet you too.

Daisuke: Wait a second, Masashi, you're holding on to his hand too much! Why don't we stop talking here in the entrance and go inside?

Miho: OK. Mark, make sure take your shoes off here.

Mark: Oh, my bad. I was about to go inside with my shoes on.

Miho: Masashi, you live in **Nakano**, right?

Masashi: Uh-huh. As a matter of fact, my apartment is real close to here. But even so, I mainly get together with Daisuke only at Ni-chome bars.

Nakano A section of Tokyo that has convenient transportation connections. Its proximity to Shinjuku Ni-chome makes it a popular area for gays to live in. In the Nakano Ward council elections of 2007, one candidate, Wataru Ishizaka (1976-), was openly gay.

まさしさん、手を握りすぎですよ

8月の、とある金曜日の夕方。
中野にある大輔のアパートに、美穂とマークがやってくる。

美穂：こんにちは！
大輔：いらっしゃい。まさしさん、すごくはりきってるよ。
まさし：余計なこと言わないの！　美穂ちゃん、こんにちは。あら！そちらがマーク？
美穂：はい。マーク、こちらが私の大学時代の友達の大輔くん。そして、お隣が、新宿二丁目を案内してくださるまさしさんです。
マーク：はじめまして。お会いできて嬉しいです。
大輔：はじめまして、大輔です。
まさし：まさしです。アタシも会えて嬉しいわ。
大輔：ちょっとまさしさん、手、握りすぎですよ。玄関先で立ち話もなんだし、とりあえず中に入って。
美穂：はい。マーク、靴はここで脱いでね。
マーク：ああ、いけない。うっかりそのまま上がってしまうところでした。
美穂：まさしさんも確か**中野**★に住んでるんですよね？
まさし：そう。実はすぐ近所のマンション。なのに大輔とはもっぱら、二丁目のバーでしか会わないのよ。

中野……東京都の特別区の一つ。交通の便が良く、新宿二丁目にも近いため、ゲイが多く住んでいるといわれている。2007年に行われた中野区議会議員選挙には、石坂わたるが、ゲイであることをカミングアウトして出馬した。

Dialog 2

Actually, it's Japanese guys I like.

Daisuke: Mark, you're living in New York now, isn't that right? Do you live with your parents?

Mark: Nope, my family lives in Boston.

Masashi: I guess if you're living alone in New York, you must be enjoying gay life to the hilt, right?

Mark: Actually, it's Japanese guys I like. But the truth is I can hardly find any over there who are on the same wavelength as me.

Miho: When I was in the States, he always hung out with me.

Masashi: You like Japanese guys ... so I guess that puts me in your range, right?

Daisuke: What a load of bull.

Masashi: You shut up.

Mark: You two seem to get along well! Where did you first get to know each other?

Daisuke: At the first gay bar I went to, five years ago. I was a bit blown over by his **"o-né" (queenie) language**, but he did give me a lot of advice about the gay world.

Masashi: After all, you were in a shaky situation——in a daze. Now look at you, so cheeky!

Daisuke: I'm still grateful to Masashi despite all this.

"o-né" (queenie) language A style of speaking primarily used among gay men in Japan, but by no means spoken by all gay men. Special words and intonation are used. The same trend can be seen with gays in English and other foreign languages. Incidentally, the word "o-né" (originally meaning older sister) refers to queenie gays.

実は日本の男の子が好きなんです

大輔のアパートで話す4人。マークが自己紹介をし、
大輔はマークに、まさしと知り合ったきっかけを説明する。

大輔：マークは今、ニューヨークに住んでいるんだよね？　ご両親も一緒に？

マーク：いえ、実家はボストンです。

まさし：ニューヨークで一人暮らしなんて、ゲイライフを満喫しまくってるんじゃない？

マーク：実は僕、日本の男の子が好きなんです。でも、話の合う人が、あまり周りにいないんですよ。

美穂：私が向こうにいる間は、私とばかり遊んでたしね。

まさし：日本人好き……。じゃあ、アタシもマークの好みの範囲内ってことね。

大輔：そんな乱暴な。

まさし：うるさい。

マーク：仲がいいんですね。二人はどこで知り合ったんですか？

大輔：5年前、僕が初めて飲みに行ったゲイバーで。最初は**おネエ言葉★**に圧倒されたけど、ゲイの世界について、いろいろアドバイスしてもらったんだ。

まさし：だってアンタ、ボーっとしてて危なっかしくて。それが今じゃ、すっかり生意気になっちゃって……。

大輔：これでも、まさしさんには本当に感謝してるんですよ。

おネエ言葉……主にゲイ男性の間で話される女言葉だが、全てのゲイがおネエ言葉を話すわけではない。言葉遣いやイントネーションに特徴があり、英語をはじめ各国の言語に、「おネエ言葉」的なものは存在する。ちなみに「おネエ」は、女性的なゲイのこと。

Dialog 3

When did you come out?

Daisuke: By the way, when did you **come out** to Miho, Mark?

Mark: About two months after we first met.

Masashi: Miho, weren't you surprised?

Miho: There were a few other gay guys at my university in New York, so I wasn't all that surprised.

Mark: Daisuke, when did you come out to Miho?

Daisuke: After she got back from New York. I thought it would be OK to tell her.

Miho: Since I was always hanging out with Mark in New York, I wonder if I've taken on an aura that attracts gays.

Masashi: Hey Miho, you better watch out! If you always hang out with gay guys, you might go too far to the other side! Get a boyfriend before getting too involved (in the gay world)! It might be too late already.

Miho: Don't say such an unlucky thing!

Masashi: Well, let's not stand here talking all day. It's about time we go to Ni-chome.

Daisuke: You're right. Shall we go?

---

come out   An abbreviation of the phrase "to come out of the closet," originally in the sense of a member of a sexual minority announcing his or her sexuality. However, in Japan nowadays, the word "come out" has come to mean more broadly "revealing one's secret."

カミングアウトはいつ？

大輔がマークに、「いつ美穂にカミングアウトしたの？」と尋ねる。
またマークも大輔に、同じ質問を投げかける。

大輔：ところでマークは、いつ美穂に**カミングアウト**★したの？

マーク：知り合ってから、2ヶ月くらい後ですね。

まさし：美穂ちゃん、びっくりしなかった？

美穂：ニューヨークの大学では、他にも何人かゲイの子がいたので、あまり驚きませんでした。

マーク：大輔が美穂にカミングアウトしたのは、いつですか？

大輔：美穂がニューヨークから帰ってから。この子なら、言っても大丈夫かな、と思って。

美穂：ニューヨークでずっとマークと遊んでいたから、ゲイウェルカムなオーラがにじみ出ちゃったのかしら。

まさし：アンタねえ、あまりゲイとばかり遊んでいると、どんどん縁遠くなるわよ！ 深入りするのは、まず彼氏を作ってからにしなさい！ もう手遅れかもしれないけど。

美穂：そんな不吉なこと、言わないでください……。

まさし：さて、ここでずっと話しているのもなんだし、そろそろ二丁目に行かない？

大輔：そうだね。じゃあ、出かけますか。

カミングアウト……coming out of closet の略で、もともとは「セクシュアルマイノリティが、自分のセクシュアリティを告白すること」を意味する隠語。しかし日本では今、広く「自分の秘密を告白すること」の意味で使用されるようになっている。

Dialog 4

What's a "o-bon" vacation?

Daisuke: This is Shinjuku Station.

Mark: There sure are a lot of people, and a lot of feverish activity.

Daisuke: Still, it seems there are fewer people than normal weekends. That's because some companies have already started their "o-bon" (summer) vacation, like mine.

Mark: What's a "o-bon" vacation?

Miho: In the summer, Japan has a festival or event called **"o-bon"** for honoring ancestors. And most companies take their summer vacations in mid-August around the "o-bon" period. So a lot of people use their off-time then to go back to their hometowns and pay visits to their ancestors' graves.

Daisuke: In the past few years, the Tokyo Pride Parade and the Tokyo Rainbow Festival have been held during the "o-bon" period.

Mark: How come? It's so hot!

Daisuke: If they are held then, it makes it easier people from outside of Tokyo to come, since they can take advantage of their holiday time.

"o-bon" In the old lunar calendar, a series of festivals and events honoring ancestral spirits fell every July 15 (around August 15 in the solar calendar). During this period, it is believed that one's ancestors actually come back home. Though each region of Japan has a different way of celebrating it, there are frequently "Bon-odori" dances, and welcome and farewell bonfires.

お盆休み？

新宿駅に到着した4人。大輔たちはマークに、お盆や、
この時期にパレードやレインボー祭りが開催される理由について説明する。

大輔：ここが新宿駅だよ。

マーク：人が多いですね。それに、すごい熱気。

大輔：でも、いつもの週末よりはすいているんじゃないかな。うちの会社みたいに、もう**お盆**★休みに入っているところもあるだろうし。

マーク：お盆休み？

美穂：日本には「お盆」という、祖先を祀る行事があるの。そしてほとんどの会社が、お盆前後の8月半ばを夏休みにしているのね。だから、その休みを利用して田舎に帰り、お墓参りをする人が多いの。

大輔：東京のパレードや東京レインボー祭りは、ここ数年、お盆の時期に開催されてるんだ。

マーク：どうして？　こんなに暑いのに！

大輔：この時期に開催すれば、東京以外の人も休みを利用して来やすいからね。

お盆……旧暦の7月15日（新暦では8月15日頃）を中心に日本で行われる、祖先の霊を祀る一連の行事。この時期には、祖先の霊が家に帰ってくると考えられている。地方によって内容は違うが、盆踊りや、迎え火、送り火などが行われることが多い。

Dialog 5

Hey, there's an "o-nakama"!

Daisuke: This is Shinjuku Avenue. If you keep on walking along this road, you'll reach Shinjuku Ni-chome.

Masashi: Hey, there's an "o-nakama" (one of us)!

Daisuke: Yeah, you could say that again. Look at that cap, those knickers, and that body. So **"ikanimo-kei" (someone obviously gay)**!

Mark: When you say "o-nakama," do you mean he's gay?

Daisuke: Yeah. It's a kind of Japanese slang, I suppose. Gays here call other gays "o-nakama" (one of us), or "kumiai no hito" (member of the union) or "kottchi no hito" (someone "on this side"). At any rate, older gays tend to use those terms.

Masashi: What the heck is that supposed to mean: "older"! What do you (younger) guys say then?

Daisuke: We usually just say "he's gay" or something like that....

Mark: So how do you say "heterosexual" in Japanese?

Masashi: We generally say "nonke."

Mark: "Nonke," huh. I'd better remember that.

Daisuke: I don't think you'll have much opportunity to use it, though!

"Ikanimo-kei" (**someone obviously gay**) Literally, someone who is "ikanimo" (obviously, indeed) gay. And "-kei" means "type." So "Ikanimo-kei" means an "obviously-gay type." Another term for it is "ikahomo." It usually has a positive connotation. Recently, many gays, when asked what type of guy they like, will answer "ikanimo-kei."

あら、お仲間さん発見！

新宿二丁目に向かって、新宿通りを歩く4人。
「日本のゲイが、同性愛者や異性愛者をどう呼ぶか」が話題になる。

大輔：ここは新宿通り。この道をまっすぐ行けば、新宿二丁目に着くんだ。

まさし：あら、お仲間さん発見！

大輔：本当だ。キャップにハーフパンツにあのガタイ。超**イカニモ系**★……。

マーク：「お仲間さん」って、ゲイのことですか？

大輔：うん。日本語のスラングと言ったらいいのかな。ゲイがゲイを指して「お仲間」とか「組合の人」とか「こっちの人」って言うんだ。まあ、年配の人が使うことが多いんだけどね。

まさし：何ですって！ じゃ、アンタたちは何ていうのよ！

大輔：いや、普通に「あの子、ゲイだね」とか……。

マーク：では、異性愛者のことは、日本語で何と言うんですか？

まさし：アタシたちは大体、「ノンケ」って言ってるわよね。

マーク：「ノンケ」ですか。覚えておこう。

大輔：あまり使う機会ないと思うけど……。

イカニモ系……文字通り、いかにもゲイっぽい人のことを指す。「イカホモ」ということもある。肯定的な意味で使われることが多く、近年、「好きなタイプは？」と聞かれ、「イカニモ系」と答えるゲイが増えている。

Dialog 6

How about a Japanese "izakaya" pub?

Mark: That's an interesting-looking building.

Daisuke: It's a theater for variety show, and is called **Shinjuku Suehiro-tei**. You can watch "rakugo" (sit-down story-telling), "manzai" (stand-up comedy dialogue), and "kijutsu" (magic tricks) there, among other things.

Mark: Sounds neat.

Daisuke: I've never been inside, though.

Masashi: Incidentally, there are a few gay bars around here, too. Their number has increased lately, with some having moved from Ni-chome. Actually, the first gay bars in Shinjuku weren't in Ni-chome, but in San-chome, I hear.

Mark: Is that so?

Masashi: Shall we eat first? It'll be a while until the bars open anyway, so how about a Japanese "izakaya" pub?

Miho: Good! It will probably be Mark's first time to experience a Japanese-style pub as well.

Masashi: So it's decided then!

Shinjuku Suehiro-tei   An entertainment hall hosting Japanese traditional variety shows. Founded in 1897 in Shinjuku San-chome, located in the block next to Ni-chome the place burnt down in World War Two, but was rebuilt in 1946. The program and performers change every ten days.

居酒屋なんてどうかしら？

新宿二丁目の手前、地下鉄の新宿三丁目駅付近にたどりついた4人。
まさしが居酒屋で食事をしようと提案する。

マーク：面白い建物がありますね。
大輔：「**新宿末廣亭★**」という寄席だよ。落語や漫才、奇術なんかが見られるんだ。
マーク：面白そうですね。
大輔：僕も、まだ入ったことはないんだけどね。
まさし：ちなみに、この辺にも、ゲイバーが何軒かあるのよ。二丁目から引っ越してくるお店もあって、最近少しずつ増えているの。そもそも、新宿で最初のゲイバーができたのは、二丁目ではなく、三丁目だったらしいわ。
マーク：そうなんですか。
まさし：先に、ご飯でも食べない？　お店が開くまでまだ時間があるし。居酒屋なんてどうかしら？
美穂：いいですね。マークも、日本風の居酒屋は初めてだろうし。
まさし：じゃあ、決まりね！

新宿末廣亭……新宿三丁目にある落語、漫才、奇術などの芸が行われている寄席。1897年創業で、第二次世界大戦により焼失したが、1946年に再建された。演目や出演者は、10日ごとに入れ替わる。

Dialog 7

It's fun, like being in a hide-out.

Mark: It's the first time for me to eat in such a small room.
Masashi: Ha-ha, are you surprised? This is a new fad in Japan recently——private room bars at **Japanese "izakaya" pubs**!
Daisuke: But Mark's so tall ... don't you feel cramped?
Mark: I'm OK. It's fun, like being in a hide-out.
Masashi: Told you! He's having fun, isn't he? I always make the right choices!
Mark: What's this small electronic terminal here?
Miho: It's for making your order with. You can also play games or have your fortune told.
Mark: That's wonderful! Everything is computerized in Japan. The menu has pictures, so it's easy to understand.
Masashi: But isn't a lot of the food new to you? Let me know if you're interested in anything. I'll explain it to you.

Japanese "izakaya" pubs A kind of eating place unique to Japan, with alcoholic drinks forming the core of the menu, but with relatively large amounts of food served as well. In recent years, a growing number of such establishments have created private rooms for customers, separating the seating areas with walls or curtains, creating a "hideout" effect.

隠れ家みたいで楽しいですね

新宿三丁目にある居酒屋で食事をする4人。
居酒屋に初めて入ったマークは、隠れ家風の個室や電子端末などに興味津々。

マーク:こんなに小さな部屋で食事をするのは初めてです。
まさし:ふふ、驚いた？　これが、最近日本で流行っている、個室タイプの**居酒屋★**よ！
大輔:でも、マーク、背が高いし……。窮屈じゃない？
マーク:大丈夫です。隠れ家みたいで楽しいですね。
まさし:ほら、喜んでるじゃない。アタシの選択に間違いはないのよ！
マーク:この、小さな端末は何ですか？
美穂:これで料理を注文するの。ゲームや占いもできるのよ。
マーク:すごい！　日本は何でも電子化されているんですね。メニューにも写真がついていて、わかりやすいです。
まさし:でも、見たことのない食べ物ばかりじゃない？　気になるものがあったら、聞いてね。説明するから。

居酒屋……酒類の提供を中心としつつ、比較的ボリュームのある料理も出す、日本独特の飲食店。近年、座席を壁やカーテンなどで細かく仕切り、個室にした「隠れ家風居酒屋」が増えている。

Dialog 8

"Niku-jaga" is the best weapon to catch a guy.

Mark : What's this?

Miho : It's "niku-jaga," a typical Japanese home-style dish, with potatoes, carrots, onions, and beef stewed in soy sauce, sweet cooking sake, and sugar, etc.

Masashi : In Japan, "niku-jaga" is the best weapon to catch a guy. Women make it (for a guy) and then try to sell themselves as a "good homemaker."

Daisuke : Does that strategy really work?

Masashi : Sure it does! Even I have used it to catch several guys so far!

Daisuke : I wonder if that's really true.

Masashi : You clam up! You sorry excuse for a fag—— you can't even handle a knife right! Oh, Mark, you listening? You're a little drunk!

Mark : It's my first time to drink **Japanese sake**. It sure tastes delicious!

Masashi : That won't do, getting so drunk this early. The evening has just begun! Here, drink some water to dilute the alcohol!

Japanese sake   A traditional form of Japanese alcoholic beverage made from fermented rice. Each region of Japan has several famous local brands. They are classified into three types according to the manufacturing method and the ingredients used "daiginjo-shu," "ginjo-shu," and "junmai-shu."

肉じゃがは、男を落とす最強兵器よ

居酒屋で食事をする4人。大輔たちは、肉じゃがについて一生懸命説明するが、日本酒を飲んで酔い始めたマークは、あまりちゃんと聞いていない。

マーク：これは何ですか？

美穂：肉じゃがよ。じゃがいも、にんじん、玉ねぎ、牛肉を、醤油やみりん、砂糖などで煮込んだもので、日本の代表的な家庭料理なの。

まさし：日本では、肉じゃがは、男を落とす最強兵器よ。女たちはこれを作って、「アタシって家庭的な女でしょ」ってアピールするの。

大輔：そんな手、通用するんですか？

まさし：するわよ！　アタシだって、今まで何人の男を落としてきたか……。

大輔：本当かなあ。

まさし：おだまり！　包丁も満足に握れない、できそこないのオカマが！　ていうかマーク、聞いてんの？　アンタちょっと飲みすぎ！

マーク：**日本酒**★って初めて飲むけど、美味しいですね。

まさし：だめよ、今からそんなに酔っ払っちゃ。夜はこれからなんだから。ほら、水飲んでアルコール薄めて！

日本酒……米を発酵させて作る、日本の伝統的な酒。日本各地にさまざまな銘柄があり、製法や原料によって、「大吟醸酒」「吟醸酒」「純米酒」などに分けられる。

Dialog 9

Can women go inside gay bars?

Masashi : Anyway, Daisuke, how about if we go to "ISLANDS" first?
Daisuke : Good idea.
Mark : What kind of place is that?
Masashi : You could say it's a standard Japanese gay bar, with a "**master**" in charge, and with karaoke.
Daisuke : It's the first gay bar I ever went to. The masters, Shima and Raku, are nice. I got to know Masashi at "ISLANDS."
Masashi : It's right near here, so I thought it would be good for our first stop.
Daisuke : But I thought women weren't allowed inside there!
Miho : What?! What should I do? Shall I wait somewhere else for a while?
Masashi : The night is still young, so there shouldn't be any problem, unless there's a customer there already who has a big problem with girls. Let me ask the master to let you in.

"master" The manager of a gay bar, usually one who is masculine both in language usage and appearance. In contrast, a bar manager who is feminine and who uses queenie language skillfully is called a "mama." That does not necessarily mean, however, that he cross-dresses.

ゲイバーって女性も入れるの？

最初に行くゲイバーは「アイランド」という店に決まるが、
美穂は、女性が入っても大丈夫かどうか、心配そう。

まさし：ところで大輔、一軒目は「アイランド」でいいわよね？
大輔：そうですね。
マーク：どんなお店なんですか？
まさし：オーソドックスな日本のゲイバー、といったらいいのかしら。マスターがいて、カラオケがあって。
大輔：僕が初めて行ったゲイバーが、そこなんだ。**マスター★**のシマさんとラクさんが、親切で。まさしさんとも「アイランド」で知り合ったんだよ。
まさし：すぐ近くにある店だし、最初に行くにはいいかな、と思って。
大輔：でもあそこ、女の子は入れないんじゃなかったっけ？
美穂：ええ!?　どうしよう。私、どこかで時間つぶしていようか？
まさし：まだ早い時間だし、よほど女の子が苦手なお客さんがいない限り、たぶん大丈夫。マスターにはアタシからお願いしてみる！

マスター……ゲイバーの店長のこと。言葉遣いや外見がどちらかといえば男性的な店長は「マスター」と呼ばれることが多い。一方、女性的だったり、巧みなおネエ言葉を話したりする店長は「ママ」と呼ばれるが、決して女装しているわけではない。

Dialog 10

That's where people who like to cross-dress get together.

Miho : Oh ... a cross-dresser just came out of that place. Is that a gay bar, too?

Masashi : No, it's a little bit different. That's where people who like to cross-dress get together.

Mark : You mean they're drag queens?

Masashi : Unh-unh, not drag queens. They don't earn money dressed up as women, and don't go up on stage. They're purely in it for personal reasons, no more, no less. We call them **"shumi-jo"** (**hobby women**).

Mark : Are they gay?

Masashi : Of course, there are transvestites who are gays, too, but there are quite a lot of straight men who cross-dress as well.

Miho : Really!? Is that a fact?

Masashi : There are several other establishments like this one, renting out lockers and costumes to guys who want to cross-dress. They wear suits on their way back from work, and they deposit their belongings in the lockers, after which they suddenly transform into women, going out on the town, drinking and so forth.

"shumi-jo" (hobby women)   An abbreviation of a Japanese phrase meaning a man who dresses up as a woman for a hobby ("shumi"). Unlike drag queens, with their over-the-board makeup, the aim of "shumi-jo" is to look like as normal a woman as possible. Some just wear female wigs and clothes without putting any makeup on their faces.

ここは、女装をしたい人が集まるお店よ

「アイランド」へ向かう途中で、美穂が変わった店を見つける。
まさしに「女装をしたい人が集まる店」だと教えられ、驚く美穂とマーク。

美穂：あ……。今、あのお店から、女装した男の人が出てきた。あそこもゲイバーなの？

まさし：うーん、ちょっと違うわね。あそこは、女装をしたい人が集まるお店よ。

マーク：ドラァグクイーンのこと？

まさし：ううん、ドラァグクイーンじゃないわ。彼らは別に、女性の格好で働いたりステージに立ったりするわけではないの。「あくまでも個人的に、女装を楽しむ男性」なのよ。アタシたちは「趣味女★」と呼んでいるわ。

マーク：彼らは、ゲイなんですか？

まさし：もちろんゲイもいるとは思うけど、ノンケの男性が結構多いみたい。

美穂：ええ!?　そうなんですか？

まさし：こういったお店は何軒かあって、女装したい人に、ロッカーや衣装を貸し出したりもしているの。彼らは会社帰りにスーツでお店に来て、ロッカーに荷物を預けて、束の間、女装して、お酒を飲んだり街を歩いたりするのよ。

趣味女……「趣味で女装している人」の略。過度なメイクを施すドラァグクイーンとは違い、目指すのはあくまでも「普通の女性」風。中には、女性用のウィッグと服を身につけただけで、顔はノーメイク、という人もいる。

Column 1

ゴールデン街にもある レズビアンやゲイの店

There are also lesbian and gay establishments in Shinjuku Golden-Gai.

新宿ゴールデン街は、新宿区歌舞伎町にある、花園神社に隣接した飲食店街です。数本の路地沿いに、木造の長屋が並び、そこで現在170軒ほどの飲食店が営業しています。

1960年代から、ゴールデン街には作家や漫画家、演劇関係者などの文化人が集まり、その中から作家の佐木隆三や中上健次、歌手の藤圭子など、さまざまなスターが登場しました。

新宿二丁目に近いことから、ゴールデン街を訪れる、あるいはゴールデン街に店を出すレズビアンやゲイも、少なからずいるようです。

一時期は「衰退していくのではないか」と危ぶまれたゴールデン街ですが、最近、若い世代からも注目されるようになり、再び活気を取り戻しつつあります。

Shinjuku Golden-Gai (Golden quarter) is an area full of drinking establishments in Kabuki-cho, lying behind the Hanazono Shrine. Along several small alleys one can find around 170 different such places, operating inside old wooden row houses.

Since the 1960s, Golden-Gai has been a favorite haunt among literary persons, such as authors, "manga" comic artists and dramatists, many of whom have gone on to gain stardom, such as the novelists Ryuzo Saki (1937-) and Kenji Nakagami (1946-92), as well as the singer Keiko Fuji (1951-). Quite a few lesbians and gays drop in on Golden-Gai because of its proximity to Ni-chome. There are also quite a lot of lesbians and gays opening their own establishments there, it seems.

At one time, it was feared that Golden-Gai would go downhill, but recently it has grabbed the attention of the younger generation, and is now gradually restoring its vitality.

Scene 2

Everything is a first for me.

何もかもが、初体験

Dialog 1

The sign "Members only" indicates a gay bar!?

Daisuke: This is a bar called "ISLANDS". We're in Shinjuku San-chome now.

Masashi: It doesn't seem so crowded yet.

Mark: What does that white sign say?

Daisuke: It says "Members only."

Miho: Really!? You have to be some sort of member to get in?

Masashi: No, no. That sign's up there to stop straight people from coming in by mistake. That sign is usually posted by gay bars everywhere, not just in Ni-chome, but also throughout Japan.

Miho: Oh, I see. It's a sort of visual marker that only gays will understand.

Mark: Something like the **rainbow flag**?

Daisuke: Well, that's a little different, I think.

Masashi: Also, not every establishment posting that kind of sign is a gay bar, either. There are some bars in places like Ginza that are truly "members-only," so you have to be careful. Anyway, shall we go in?

---

rainbow flag Since a rainbow has many colors coexisting with each other in an equal status, it has been adopted in the rainbow flag to represent diversity and equality. The flag is often used as a symbol of LGBTs, as well as LGBT-friendly corporations and groups.

「会員制」はゲイバーの目印!?

「アイランド」に到着した4人。入り口に貼ってある「会員制」の札に
目を留めるマークに、「それはゲイバーの目印だ」と教えるまさし。

大輔:ここが「アイランド」だよ。

まさし:まだそんなに混んでなさそうね。

マーク:この白い札には、なんと書いてあるんですか?

大輔:「会員制」だよ。

美穂:ええ!? 何かの会員じゃないと入れないんですか?

まさし:違う違う。これは、ノンケのお客さんが間違って入ってくるのを防ぐために貼ってあるの。二丁目に限らず、日本全国どの地域に行っても、たいていのゲイバーにはこの札が貼ってあるわね。

美穂:なるほど。ゲイだけにわかる、ゲイバーの目印ってことですね。

マーク:**レインボーフラッグ**★みたいなものかな?

大輔:うーん、それとはちょっと違う気がする……。

まさし:ただ、これが貼ってある店が全部ゲイバーってわけじゃないの。銀座あたりに行けば、本物の「会員制」の店もあると思うから、気をつけてね。じゃ、中に入るわよ。

レインボーフラッグ……虹にはさまざまな色が共存していることから、レインボーフラッグは「多様性・平等性」を示しているとされる。LGBTの象徴として、あるいはLGBTフレンドリーな企業や団体の目印として使われることも多い。

Dialog 2

Mark, you're gay, too, right?

Raku : Masashi and Daisuke, welcome.

Masashi : Thanks. It's quite hot out, so this **"oshibori" towel** feels good.

Daisuke : Oh, you're wiping your face with the "oshibori?"

Masashi : Anything wrong with that? (Note: women in Japan don't like to wipe their faces with "oshibori" as it would ruin their makeup.)

Raku : You two are here for the first time, right?

Miho : Yes. I'm Miho. Nice to meet you.

Mark : I'm Mark. I came here on vacation from the United States.

Raku : How do you do, I'm Raku. How did you get to know these two, Daisuke?

Daisuke : Miho is my friend from college days, and Mark is Miho's friend. Mark wanted to see a bar in Ni-chome, so we're showing him around.

Raku : Oh, is that so? Mark, you're gay, too, right? It's your first time in a Japanese gay bar?

Mark : Yes.

"oshibori" towel   Given out at eating and drinking establishments, the "oshibori" towel is a custom unique to Japan. There are those made of cloth (dipped in water), and those made of paper and/or bonded-fiber fabric. "Oshibori" can be either hot or cold. Many gay bars use rental "oshibori" services.

マークさんもゲイなんですよね？

「アイランド」の店内にて。おしぼりを運んできたマスターのラクに、
美穂とマークを紹介し、今までのいきさつを説明する大輔。

ラク：まさし、大輔、いらっしゃい。
まさし：ありがとう。暑いから、**おしぼり**★が気持ちいい。
大輔：あ、おしぼりで顔拭いてる……。
まさし：何よ、文句ある？
ラク：……お二人は、初めてですよね？
美穂：はい。美穂です。はじめまして。
マーク：僕はマークです。アメリカから遊びに来ました。
ラク：はじめまして、ラクです。大輔は、お二人とはどうやって知り合ったの？
大輔：美穂は僕の大学時代の友だちで、マークは美穂の友だちなんです。マークが二丁目のバーに行きたがっていたので、僕らが案内することになったんですよ。
ラク：へえ、そうなんだ。マークさんもゲイなんですね？ 日本のゲイバーは初めて？
マーク：はい。

おしぼり……飲食店などで使用される手を拭く道具で、日本特有のもの。タオル地の布を水に浸してしぼったもの、紙や不織布を用いた使い捨てタイプのものなどがある。ゲイバーなどでは、レンタル業者を使っているところも多い。

Dialog 3

So, we'll have four "chuhai" mixed with Oolong tea.

Raku: What will you have to drink?

Masashi: Use my "keep" (reserved) bottle. Oh, maybe I have a **"chance bottle"** (my bottle's getting low)?

Raku: Yes.

Masashi: Oh, no, what should I do?! Well, anyway, give me a new one then. By the way, Mark, have you ever drunk "shochu" (Japanese vodka-like distilled spirits)?

Mark: Nope, it's my first time.

Masashi: We usually drink it as "chuhai" (mixed "shochu") with Oolong tea, but maybe you would prefer it mixed with acerola (a sweet, fruity juice)?

Mark: I'm not sure, but I'll just have what everyone else is having.

Masashi: OK, we'll have four "chuhai" with Oolong tea then.

Raku: Yes, sir.

Masashi: Hey, Mark, how come you have your wallet out? You pay when you leave!

Mark: Is that so? Japanese gay bars are quite interesting: you can talk with the "master" about various things, and you don't have to pay cash on delivery.

"chance bottle" A Japlish term meaning a "keep" (reserved) bottle that is getting low. Incidentally, it costs around 4,000 yen to purchase a "keep" bottle of Jinro (Korean shochu) at a Japanese gay bar. It costs 1,500 yen to have a drink set (drink plus side dishes), with Oolong tea mixed with the shochu from the bottle.

じゃあ、ウーロン茶割りを4つで

ラクに、自分のキープボトルを出すよう頼むまさし。
ニューヨークのバーと日本のバーのさまざまな違いに直面し、面白がるマーク。

ラク：お飲み物はどうしましょう？
まさし：アタシのボトルで。あっ、もしかして**チャンスボトル**★だった？
ラク：はい。
まさし：キャー、大変！ じゃあ、新しいの入れてください……。ところでマークは、焼酎飲んだことある？
マーク：いえ、初めてです。
まさし：アタシたちはウーロン茶割りにするけど、マークはアセロラ割りの方がいいかしら。
マーク：よくわかりませんが、みなさんと一緒でいいです。
まさし：じゃあ、ウーロン茶割りを4つで。
ラク：はい、わかりました。
まさし：ちょっとマーク、何財布出してんのよ。お金は帰る時に払うの。
マーク：そうなんですか？ マスターとはいろいろ話せるし、キャッシュオンデリバリーじゃないし、日本のゲイバーは面白いですね。

チャンスボトル……空になりそうな、客のキープボトルのこと。ちなみにゲイバーでは、ボトル1本の料金は4000円程度(真露の場合)から。ドリンク1杯(ボトルを入れた場合は、ウーロン茶等の割り物) ＋チャージのセット料金は、1500円程度。

Dialog 4

Here are your "o-toshi."

Raku: Ok, four "chuhai" with Oolong tea coming up. Here are your **"o-toshi"** (small side dishes).
Miho: They look delicious.
Mark: What are they?
Masashi: Spinach dressed with sesame, and potato salad. Raku made the dishes himself.
Mark: Japanese gay bars even serve food. That's a surprise.
Daisuke: Mark, how does your drink taste, the "shochu" mixed with Oolong tea?
Mark: Well, I'd have to say it's a little bitter. Not sure if I would say it tastes good or not.
Masashi: Anyway, "chuhai" with Oolong tea is the most "orthodox" drink served at gay bars in Japan. Since you've come all the way to this country, you ought to memorize the taste before you go back!
Mark: I see.
Daisuke: Hmm, the most "orthodox" drink ... is that really so?

"o-toshi" Food in a small bowl or on a small plate that comes with the first drink you order at a bar or "izakaya" pub. Cooked food are called "nuremono" (wet dishes), while nuts and crackers are called "kawakimono" (dry dishes).

はい、お通しよ

運ばれてきたお通しがマスターの手作りだと聞いて、驚くマーク。
また、焼酎のウーロン茶割りを初めて飲むが、味がよくわからない様子。

ラク：はい、ウーロン茶割り4つと**お通し**★。
美穂：美味しそう。
マーク：これは何ですか？
まさし：ほうれん草の胡麻和えとポテトサラダ。ラクさん手作りのお通しよ。
マーク：日本のゲイバーは、食べ物まで出すんですね。びっくりしました。
大輔：マーク、焼酎のウーロン茶割りはどんな感じ？
マーク：うーん、ちょっと苦いかな。おいしいかどうか、よくわかりません。
まさし：でも、焼酎のウーロン茶割りは、日本のゲイバーではもっともオーソドックスな飲み物なの。せっかく日本に来たんだから、この味、覚えて帰りなさい！
マーク：はい、わかりました。
大輔：もっともオーソドックスな飲み物って……。本当かなあ……。

お通し……バーや居酒屋などで酒を注文した時に出てくる、小鉢や小皿に入った食べ物。惣菜などは「濡れもの」、ナッツやクラッカーなどは「乾きもの」といわれる。

Dialog 5

Someone has started singing karaoke.

Mark: Someone has started singing **karaoke**. There are bars in New York, too, where you can sing karaoke.
Daisuke: Really, I didn't know that.
Mark: In New York bars, however, one usually gets up on stage and sings. Not like in Japan.
Daisuke: Yeah, in Japan, especially gay bars, most people sing Karaoke in their own seats, without moving.
Mark: There are also several gay bars in Greenwich Village that have pianos. Everyone sings musical numbers along with the pianist's accompaniment.
Masashi: There's a bar in Ni-chome with a piano, too, but I've never seen all the customers do a sing-along. What a shame; it would be fun to have a choral café.
Daisuke: Hmm, a choral café? Sounds fun, anyway. I'd like to visit one some time.
Mark: Come to New York, and I'll take you to one!

---

karaoke A form of entertainment invented in Japan, in which people sing along to a prerecorded accompaniment. It has since spread around the world. A lot of Japanese gay bars have online karaoke. Still, quite a few gays (and others) hate karaoke as it makes it difficult to converse with other people.

カラオケが始まりましたね

客が歌いだしたカラオケに反応するマーク。ニューヨークには、カラオケの
歌えるバーも、ピアノの演奏に合わせて客が歌うゲイバーもあるらしい。

マーク:**カラオケ★**が始まりましたね。ニューヨークにも、カラオケ
で歌えるバーがありますよ。

大輔:へえ、そうなんだ。

マーク:でも、ニューヨークでは、歌う人はステージに立つことが
多いんです。日本は違うんですね。

大輔:確かに日本の、特にゲイバーでは、自分の席で歌うことが多
いかも。

マーク:それから、グリニッチヴィレッジには何軒か、ピアノを置
いているゲイバーがあります。そこではピアニストの演奏に
合わせて、お客さんがミュージカルナンバーを合唱したりす
るんですよ。

まさし:二丁目にもピアノを置いているバーはあるけど、お客さん
の合唱ってのは、見たことがないわね。やだ、歌声喫茶み
たいで楽しそう。

大輔:歌声喫茶って……。でも、確かに楽しそうだね。その店、一
度行ってみたいなあ。

マーク:今度、是非ニューヨークに来てください。案内します！

カラオケ……あらかじめ録音された伴奏に合わせて歌う、日本発祥の娯楽文化。今では
世界各国に広まっている。日本のゲイバーの多くは通信カラオケを置いているが、中に
は「会話ができなくなる」等の理由で、カラオケを嫌っているゲイもいる。

Dialog 6

Your first crush was a "deli-hel boy"!?

Masashi: Mark, what's the matter? You're staring at that guy standing at the entrance. Oh, that's Ken'ichi.
Mark: Masashi, do you know him?
Masashi: I'm familiar with his face, that's about it.
Mark: Oh ... he put something down, and then went right away.
Masashi: That guy is a "**deli-hel boy**." Mark, tell me, is he your type?
Mark: No, but, actually....
Masashi: Come out and say it!
Mark: That guy ... he looked like the guy I fell in love with for the first time.
Masashi, Daisuke, Miho: Really?!
Mark: I thought you would laugh, so I didn't say anything. But as a matter of fact, I did come to Japan this time with the slight expectation that I might meet up with him.

"deli-hel boy" Short in Japanese for "delivery health boy," this term refers to volunteer young men who deliver condoms and awareness-campaign posters to bars, cruising spots, and various club events in Ni-chome and elsewhere. They were first organized by Rainbow Ring, an awareness group aiming at the prevention of HIV/AIDS.

デリヘルボーイが、初恋の子！？

店に入って来た男の子の顔を見て、何故かハッとするマーク。
まさしに理由を問い詰められたマークは、意外な事実を告白する。

まさし：マーク、どうしたのよ。入り口の方をじっと見て。
　　　　……あら、健一が来ているのね。
マーク：まさしさん、あの男の子と知り合いなんですか？
まさし：顔を知ってる程度だけどね。
マーク：あ……。何か置いて、すぐに帰っちゃった。
まさし：あの子、**デリヘルボーイ**★をやってるのよ。マーク、ああいう子が好みなの？
マーク：いや、実は……。
まさし：はっきり言いなさいよ。
マーク：さっきの男の子、僕の初恋の人に似ていたんです。
まさし・大輔・美穂：ええ!?
マーク：笑われそうだから黙っていたんですが……。実は今回も、「もしかしたら彼に会えるかも」と、ちょっとだけ期待して、日本に来たんです。

デリヘルボーイ……「デリバリーヘルスボーイ」の略で、二丁目のバーやハッテン場、クラブイベントなどにコンドームや啓発用ポスターを配達する、ボランティアの男の子たち。RAINBOW RING（HIV/AIDSの予防啓発等を行う団体）の呼びかけで結成された。

Dialog 7

I think he was probably gay, too.

Miho: Come to think of it, Mark, didn't you tell me before that your first crush was Japanese?

Mark: Yes. We went to the same grade school. But right before middle school began, he had to go back to Japan because of his dad's job.

Masashi: You couldn't forget your first love, so that's how you came to like Japanese guys, right?

Mark: Uh-huh.

Daisuke: Didn't you correspond with each other?

Mark: We did for a while, but then both he and I changed our addresses, so before we knew it we had lost contact with each other. Anyway, I think he was probably gay, too.

Masashi: Wow, you sure are confident about that. Don't tell me you were having sex while still in grade school?! Who was **"tachi" (top)**, and who was **"neko" (bottom)**?

Mark: W-wrong! But when we were playing together, we almost got that far sometimes.

Masashi: Ew, gross, acting like adults when still kids!

"tachi" (top) and "neko" (bottom)   Jargon referring to the division of roles in homosexual sex. "Tachi" (top) refers to the active (male) role, while "neko" or "uke" refers to the passive (female) role.

彼もたぶんゲイだったと思うんですよ

まさしたちの質問攻めにあい、徐々に初恋の思い出について話し始めるマーク。
マークの初恋の相手は、同じ小学校に通っていた、日本人の男の子だった。

美穂：そういえばマーク、前に言ってたよね。初恋の相手が日本人の男の子だったって。

マーク：はい。同じ小学校に通っていた子なんですが、中学校に上がる頃、お父さんの仕事で、日本に帰ってしまったんです。

まさし：その初恋の彼が忘れられなくて、日本人好きになっちゃったってわけ？

マーク：はい。

大輔：手紙のやりとりは、しなかったの？

マーク：しばらくはしていたんですが、僕の家も彼の家も引っ越して、いつの間にか連絡がとれなくなってしまって。……彼もたぶんゲイだったと思うんですよ。

まさし：やけに自信満々ね。まさかアンタ、小学生の分際でやっちゃったわけ？　どっちが**タチ**★でどっちが**ウケ**★よ！

マーク：ち、違います！　でも二人で遊んでいる時に、何となくその一歩手前くらいまでは……。

まさし：いやだ、このマセガキ！

タチ、ウケ……同性間のセックスにおける役割分担を示す隠語。タチは、セックスにおいて能動的な側を指し、ネコはセックスにおいて受動的な側を指す。

Dialog 8

After he finishes distributing condoms....

Masashi : Just for my information, what was his name?

Mark : Yohei Suzuki. Here's a picture of him from grade school.

Masashi : No mistake about it, he does look like Ken'ichi.... Maybe "Ken'ichi" is just his **"genji-na"** (gay alias). Let's check back with him later (to see if he might really be Yohei).

Mark : Sure, if you would!

Daisuke : Masashi, do you know Ken'ichi's whereabouts?

Masashi : Definitely! There's a community center in Ni-chome called "akta", and after he finishes distributing condoms he should be going back there. But we still have some time before that, so let's hop around a few more bars first. Who knows, we might find some other candidates for "Yohei Suzuki."

Daisuke : I sort of doubt it. I would say the chances are extremely slim to nil that Yohei is a gay guy who likes to go drinking at Ni-chome, and that he's here today at one of those particular places.

Masashi : If you give up, you won't get anywhere. What have you got to lose?!

"genji-na" Originally the aliases used by courtesans (prostitutes) in the old licensed quarters (red-light districts). From that, the term started to be used for the names——completely different from real names——used in gay bars and elsewhere by both staff members and customers. However, in recent years, the number of gays using "genji-na" has declined radically.

コンドームを配り終えたら……

マークの初恋話を聞き終えた大輔たちは、マークの恋に協力することに。
「面倒見のいいおネエさん」の血が騒ぐのか、やけにはりきっているまさし。

まさし：ちなみに、その子の名前は？
マーク：スズキヨウヘイ君でした。これが小学生の頃の写真です。
まさし：確かに、健一に似てるわね……。「健一」ってのは**源氏名**★かもしれないし、後で本人に確かめてみましょう。
マーク：はい、よろしくお願いします！
大輔：まさしさん、健一君の居場所知ってるんですか？
まさし：当然よ！ 二丁目に「akta」っていうコミュニティセンターがあるんだけど、コンドームを配り終えたら、そこに戻るはずよ。ただ、それまでまだ時間があるから、別の店を何軒か回らない？ もしかしたら他にも、スズキヨウヘイの候補者が出てくるかもしれないし。
大輔：それはどうかなあ。ヨウヘイくんが二丁目に飲みに行くゲイで、しかも今日、この辺りに来ている可能性なんて、限りなく低いと思うけど……。
まさし：あきらめたら、何も始まらないじゃない。ダメでもともとよ！

源氏名……もともとは、遊女の遊郭内での名前のこと。転じてゲイバーなどでは、従業員や客が名乗る、本名とは全く違う名前を意味する。しかし昔に比べると、源氏名を使うゲイの数は、かなり減っている。

Dialog 9

Are they all gay?

Daisuke: Ni-chome starts on the other side of this street.
Mark: We're finally there. I'm really looking forward to it.
Masashi: Oh, that reminds of the first time I ever set foot in Ni-chome. When I crossed this street, I was trembling with expectation and anxiety and tension, telling myself, "I'm finally going to go to a gay town now."
Daisuke: Masashi, you're getting a distant look in your eyes.
Masashi: By the way, the building you see just as you cross the street is the **BYGS Building**.
Mark: There are a lot of people grouped near the entrance. Are they all gay?
Masashi: I think so, probably. The BYGS Building is something of a landmark in Ni-chome, so it's often used as a meeting spot.
Daisuke: Landmark...? That's overstating it a bit, I think.
Masashi: What are you muttering about? Let's go!

BYGS Building   An office building near the exit of the Shinjuku San-chome subway station, with 13 stories above ground and two basement floors. It contains various tenants, including the interior shop "ACTUS" and the Japanese pub "Uoya Iccho". A lot of lesbians and gays frequent these places.

あれはみんなゲイなのかな？

「アイランド」を出て、二丁目へ向かう4人。
三丁目と二丁目の間にある通りの前で、過去を思い出し、突然感慨にふけるまさし。

大輔：この通りの向こうが二丁目だよ。
マーク：いよいよですね。とても楽しみです。
まさし：ああ、思い出すわ……。初めて二丁目に来た日は、この通りを渡る時に「いよいよこれからゲイの街に行くんだわ」って、期待と不安と緊張に震えたものよ……。
大輔：まさしさん、遠い目になってますよ。
まさし：ちなみに、横断歩道を渡ってすぐ前にあるのが、BYGSビル★。
マーク：入り口付近に人が集まっていますね。あれはみんな、ゲイなのかな？
まさし：たぶんそうだと思うわ。BYGSビルは、二丁目のランドマークみたいなものだから、よく待ち合わせなんかに使われるのよ。
大輔：ランドマークって……。そんな大げさなものじゃないと思うけど。
まさし：何、ぶつぶつ言ってんの。行くわよ！

BYGSビル……地下鉄新宿三丁目駅の出口付近にある、地下2階、地上13階建てのオフィスビル。インテリアショップ「アクタス」や、居酒屋「うおや一丁」などがテナントとして入居しており、レズビアンやゲイの利用者も多い。

Dialog 10

I hear there's about 200 to 300 gay-related places.

Daisuke: This street is called "Naka-dori" ——it's the main street of Ni-chome. It's still early now, so there aren't so many people around yet.

Mark: There sure are a lot of signs on the buildings. Are all these shops gay-related?

Daisuke: Not all of them, but I hear there's about 200 to 300 such places.

Mark: Wow!

Daisuke: Even so, during the daytime, Ni-chome serves as a regular business area, too.

Masashi: There are office buildings, **a theater**, **a club with live music ("live house")**, a credit union, and an elementary school as well. Anyway, the condition of the roads is better than before, and cleaner.

Mark: There's a big monitor on the side of this building.

Masashi: You can often watch advertisements for club events on it.

Mark: It must be good for publicity being so visible.

---

theater, and club with live music ("live house") "TINY ALICE" along Naka-dori is a small theater that opened in 1995. Also, "Shinjuku Pit Inn" is a long-standing club with live music (called a "live house" in Japan), where Elvin Jones (1927-2004, member of the Coltrane Quartet) used to play every year. It now has live shows by such veteran Japanese jazz musicians as Sadao Watanabe (1933-), Yosuke Yamashita (1942-), and Terumasa Hino (1942-).

200〜300軒はゲイ関係のお店らしいよ

二丁目に着いた4人は、まずメインストリートの仲通りへ。
ゲイバーの多さや、ビルの壁にかけられた大型ディスプレイに驚くマーク。

大輔:この道が仲通り。二丁目のメインストリートだよ。まだ時間が早いから、そんなに人はいないけど。

マーク:たくさん看板が並んでいますね。これが全部ゲイ関係のお店なんですか？

大輔:全部ではないけど、200〜300軒くらいは、そうだと言われているんだ。

マーク:すごい！

大輔:ただ、二丁目は、昼間はビジネス街でもあるんだよ。

まさし:オフィスビルもあれば、**劇場やライブハウス★**、信用金庫や学校もあるしね。それにしても昔に比べたら、道路も整備されて、きれいになったわよ。

マーク:そのビルの壁に、大きなディスプレイがかかっていますね。

まさし:クラブイベントの映像なんかが、よく流れているわね。

マーク:人目につくし、宣伝効果が高そうですね。

劇場やライブハウス……仲通り沿いにある「タイニイアリス」は、1995年にオープンした小劇場。また「新宿 PIT INN」は、かつてエルヴィン・ジョーンズが演奏したことがあり、渡辺貞夫や山下洋輔、日野皓正などもライブを行う、ジャズ・ライブハウスの老舗。

Column 2

二丁目にある3つのお寺
The three temples of Ni-chome

　新宿二丁目には太宗寺、成覚寺、正受院という、3つの寺院があります。太宗寺は、1596年頃に作られた僧侶・太宗の庵を前身とした寺で、1625年頃には、この太宗寺の門前に町屋ができました。境内には江戸庶民の信仰を集めた閻魔大王像や奪衣婆像、都指定文化財の銅造地蔵菩薩坐像などがあります。

　一方、成覚寺は、1595年に建てられた寺で、境内には、江戸時代の遊女の共同墓地「子供合埋碑」などがあります。成覚寺に隣接する正受院も、1594年に建てられた寺で、「咳止めに霊験がある」とされ、江戸庶民から「綿のおばば」と親しまれた奪衣婆像があります。

Shinjuku Ni-chome contains three Buddhist temples: Taiso-ji, Jokaku-ji, and Shoju-in. The first was preceded by a monastery set up by the monk Taiso in 1596, and later became a temple. Buildings and shops started to spread out before the front gate of Taiso-ji around 1625. Inside the temple grounds can be found an Emma-Daio statue and a Datsueba statue that were worshipped by common people in the Edo era. There is also a bronze seated figure of the Jizo Bosatsu that has been designated as a designated cultural property by the Tokyo Metropolitan Government.
Meanwhile, Jokaku-ji, which was built in 1595, contains the "Kodomo Gomai-hi," a common grave for courtesans (prostitutes) of the Edo era. Shoju-in stands next to Jokaku-ji, and was also built in 1594. It holds a Datsueba statue that was believed by common folk in the Edo era to work miracles against coughs, and was given the nickname "wata-no-obaba" (cotton grandmother).

Scene 3
All sorts of gay bars, all sorts of gays

ゲイバーいろいろ、ゲイもいろいろ

Dialog 1

Can a woman go in there by herself?

Masashi: Mark, how 'bout this **shot bar** "ARTY FARTY HQ?" There are several foreigners inside, and it seems to have a welcoming atmosphere that makes it easy to fit in.

Mark: Nice! This place has a mood similar to a shot bar in New York that Miho and I used to go to often.

Miho: I was thinking the same thing. By the way, there do seem to be a lot of women here.

Daisuke: Not all of them came with gay friends, either.

Miho: Can a woman go in there by herself?

Masashi: I don't see any problem. As long as you don't let your hair down too much and cause a ruckus, or create problems for the gay customers. This bar has a separate annex called "THE ANNEX" that seems to have a higher ratio of female customers.

Miho: Hmm, maybe I'll try going there some time.

Masashi: A good time might be on Saturdays, later at night. It's quite crowded then, but everyone is dancing and getting pumped up.

Miho: Sounds like fun!

---

shot bar   A place where drinks are served and paid for one at a time. There aren't any "o-toshi" side dishes served, and customers cannot reserve bottles. Also, the staff do not mix socially with the customers any more than necessary. But the drinks are quite cheap, at 500 yen a glass.

女の子だけで来てもいいのかしら？

まさしは3人を、ショットバー「ARTY FARTY HQ」へ連れて行く。
店内の様子に、昔2人で行ったニューヨークのゲイバーを思い出す、マークと美穂。

まさし：マーク、この**ショットバー**★「ARTY FARTY HQ」はどう？　外国人もいるし、なじみやすいと思ったんだけど。

マーク：いいですね！　昔、美穂と一緒に遊びに行ったニューヨークのショットバーと、雰囲気が似ています。

美穂：うん、私もそう思った。……ところでここには、女の子も結構いるのね。

大輔：みんな、ゲイの友達と一緒に遊びに来たんじゃないかな。

美穂：女の子だけで来てもいいのかしら？

まさし：大丈夫だと思うわよ。ハメを外しすぎて大騒ぎしたり、ゲイの客に迷惑をかけたりしなければ。あと、このお店には「THE ANNEX」という別館があって、そっちの方が女子率は高いみたい。

美穂：じゃあ、今度遊びに行ってみようかな。

まさし：土曜日の、少し遅めの時間なんていいかもね。かなり混んでるけど、みんな踊ってて盛り上がるし。

美穂：楽しそう！

ショットバー……お酒を一杯ずつ出してくれるお店のこと。お通しやボトルキープはなく、従業員が必要以上に接客することもないが、料金は一杯500円程度からと、安め。

Dialog 2

Is the clientele at each gay bar completely different?

Mark: Anyway, there do seem to be a lot of cute guys here.
Masashi: Just as I thought, you're a "**waka-sen**" (you prefer young guys).
Daisuke: Not really. People who might be "young" to you, Masashi, are the same age as far as Mark is concerned. So he's not really a "waka-sen," but just someone who prefers guys his own age, like most people do.
Masashi: Somehow, your language bothers me.
Miho: By the way, is the clientele at each gay bar completely different?
Masashi: Well, kind of.... There are places like this one, where a lot of young guys congregate, while others like "ISLANDS" tend to attract a broader range of customers, especially those in their 30s. There are also gay bars exclusively for older men, but most of those are in Shimbashi or Ueno or Asakusa (all in Tokyo).
Miho: So there are differences depending on geographical area, too.
Masashi: There are also "**fuke-sen**" bars (for guys with a preference for older guys). I've never been to one yet, though.
Miho: "Fuke-sen" ... that's a heckuva word!

"waka-sen," "fuke-sen" "Waka-sen" is short for "wakamono-senmon," literally someone who specializes in young guys. In contrast, "fuke-sen" is an abbreviation of "fuketa-hito senmon," or someone who likes older men. There's even a word, "oke-sen," which means a preference for extremely senior guys with one foot in the coffin, or "kan-oke." All these words are specialized jargon among gays, and not common knowledge.

ゲイバーによって、客層は全然違うの？

引き続き「ARTY FARTY HQ」店内にて。
ゲイバーの客層の違いについて解説するまさし。

マーク：それにしても、かわいい子が、たくさんいますね。
まさし：アンタ、やっぱり**若専**★なのね……。
大輔：いや、まさしさんからすれば「若い子」でも、マークにとっては同世代なんだから。若専というより、マークは普通に、同世代が好きなだけなのでは？
まさし：引っかかるわね、その言い方……。
美穂：ところでゲイバーって、お店によって、客層は全然違うの？
まさし：そうね。ここみたいに、若い子がたくさん集まるお店もあれば、「アイランド」みたいに、30代を中心に、幅広く集まるお店もあるし。年配の人ばかりが集まるお店もあるけど、そういうお店は、新橋とか上野とか浅草の方が多いわ。
美穂：地域によっても違いがあるのね。
まさし：「**老け専**★バー」というのもあるわよ。アタシもまだ、行ったことはないけど……。
美穂：老け専……。すごい言葉ね。

若専、老け専……「若専」は「若者専門」の略で、若者が好きな人のこと。「老け専」は「老けた人専門」の略で、年配の人が好きな人のこと。さらに、棺桶に足をつっこんでいるような老人が好きな人を「オケ専」という。いずれも、ゲイの間での隠語。

Dialog 3

I'll wait outside, so you guys go on ahead.

Masashi: "GB Tokyo" is where a lot of foreigners like to come. Unfortunately, it's a **"men only"** place, so we'd better forget about it today.

Miho: I'll wait outside, so you guys go on ahead.

Masashi: No way, we can't leave Miho standing outside here all alone like this! Even though this is a gay town——we can't do that!

Daisuke: Well, in that case, I'll wait with Miho around here. Mark, you came all this way, so why don't you let Masashi take you inside?

Mark: You're right. I'd like to go inside.

Masashi: Well, let's go in and take a look. Perhaps Yohei is in there!

Daisuke: Masashi, don't raise Mark's hopes up too much!

---

men only Certain gay-related establishments and clubs only allow men in. This restriction is placed when the bar manager or the organizer of an event wants to provide his customers with the kind of place where gays can feel relaxed, or where gays can meet and hit on each other.

メンオンリーだから外で待つわ

「ARTY FARTY HQ」を出た4人は、「GB Tokyo」の前を通りかかる。
メンオンリーの店であるため、まさしとマークだけが中に入ることに。

まさし：この「GB Tokyo」は、外国人がたくさん集まるお店なんだけど……。残念ながら、**メンオンリー★**なので、今日は無理ね。

美穂：私はここで待ってますから、みなさんでどうぞ。

まさし：やだ、美穂ちゃん一人、こんなところに置き去りにできないわよ！　いくらゲイの街だからって……。

大輔：じゃあ僕、美穂と一緒に、この辺で待っています。マーク、せっかくだから、まさしさんに連れて行ってもらったら？

マーク：そうですね。中に入ってみたいです。

まさし：それならちょっと、覗いてこようかしら。もしかしたら、ヨウヘイくんがいるかもしれないしね！

大輔：まさしさん、あまりマークに期待させちゃダメですよ……。

メンオンリー……店やクラブイベントなどに、男性しか入れないこと。店長やオーガナイザーが「ゲイがくつろげる場所や、ゲイ同士の出会いの場を提供したい」と思っている場合は、メンオンリーになることが多い。

Dialog 4

My friends call me a "rice queen."

Masashi: Well, say what you like, but there doesn't seem to be anyone like Yohei here after all.

Mark: I see. Anyway, this place seems easy to drop in on, even for foreigners.

Masashi: All the staff have speak pretty good Engish, too. Oh, that guy over there has been glancing at you for the past few minutes, Mark. He must be a "**gai-sen**" (someone with a fetish for foreigners, especially Westerners). Mark, is there the concept of "gai-sen" in the States, too?

Mark: Yes, my friends call me a "rice queen."

Masashi: What does that mean?

Mark: It means a (Western) gay who likes Asians. Incidentally, (Asian) gays who only date with whites are called "potato queens."

Masashi: Oh, I didn't know that.

Mark: However, to become a rice queen (you have to suffer) the prejudice of some people who feel you're simply a white guy that other whites shun (and thus choose Asians instead). As a matter of fact, when you go to Asian (gay) bars, also, you see a lot older whites coupled with younger Asians.

Masashi: Yeah, that would feel a little bit awkward, for sure.

"gai-sen" Short for "gaijin-senmon," it refers to a Japanese gay who prefers foreigners ("gaijin"). However, it does not mean all types of foreigners, but mainly whites or blacks from the West. Recently, though, there are more and more Japan who like other Asians, especially from countries like Taiwan, Korea and Thailand. Other bars that are well-known hangouts for foreigners and "gai-sen"are "Fuji"and "DraGon."

僕は友達から「ライスクイーン」といわれています

「GB Tokyo」の店内にて。
「外専」はアメリカでどう表現されるかを説明するマーク。

まさし：とはいったものの、やっぱり、ヨウヘイくんらしい子はいないわね。

マーク：はい……。でもこのお店は、外国人でも、気楽に来られますね。

まさし：お店の人、みんな英語堪能だしね。あら、あの子、マークのこと、さっきからチラチラ見てるわよ。きっと**外専**★ね。マーク、アメリカにも「外専」という概念はあるの？

マーク：はい。僕は友達から「ライスクイーン」といわれています。

まさし：それはどういう意味？

マーク：アジア人好きなゲイ、という意味ですね。ちなみに、白人しか相手にしない人は、「ポテトクイーン」といわれるんです。

まさし：へえ、そうなんだ。

マーク：でも「ライスクイーンになるのは、白人に相手にされない白人だ」という偏見が強くて。実際アジアンバーへ行くと、白人の年配の男とアジア人の若い男の子、という組み合わせが多いんですよね。

まさし：なるほど、ちょっと複雑な気分になるわね……。

外専……「外国人専門」の略で、外国人が好きな人のこと。ただし、この「外国人」は主に、欧米から来た白人や黒人を指している。一方で近年、台湾や韓国、タイなど、アジア人を好む日本人ゲイも増えている。なお「外国人や外専が集まる店」としては、他に「Fuij」「DraGon」などが有名。

Dialog 5

Oh dear, here comes a pain in the neck!

Mark: It's caught my attention for a while——there sure are a lot of people hanging around that bar there!

Masashi: Oh, that's "advocates café tokyo." Because of its **open-air café/bar** style, a lot of people gather there, especially in summer. There are a lot of foreigners, too. Oh dear, here comes a pain in the neck!

Taro: Sister Masako, it's been a while!

Masashi: Yeah, long time no see. Are you still going with that American boyfriend of yours?

Taro: Nope, we broke up long ago. Hey, this guy with you, he's super good-looking! Introduce him to me!

Masashi: I'd like to, but there's no time now. See you next time!

Taro: What the...?! Too bad! Well, at least let's exchange names with each other. How do you do? I'm Taro.

Mark: Hi, I'm Mark.

Taro: Do you live in Japan?

Mark: No, I live in New York. I'm now on a trip to Japan.

Taro: How long do you plan to stay? Tell me how to reach you, if it's all right with you.

Masashi: Hey, Mark, let's get a move on!

---

open-air café/bar A café or bar that has been set up outdoors, usually on a sidewalk or a plaza. While occasionally found in Japanese cities, there are hardly as many as in the West because of restrictive road conditions.

あら、面倒くさい子が来たわ！

再び合流し、オープンカフェスタイルのバー「advocates café tokyo」の前を
通りかかる４人。一人の男の子が話しかけてくるが、まさしは何故か冷たくあしらう。

マーク：さっきから気になっていたんですが、あのお店の前に、たくさん人がいますね。

まさし：「advocates café tokyo」ね。**オープンカフェ**★スタイルだから、夏場は特に、人が集まるのよね。外国人も多いし。あら、面倒くさい子がいるわ……。

太郎：まさ子ネエさん、お久しぶりです！

まさし：久しぶりね……。アンタ、あのアメリカ人の彼氏とは、今も続いてるの？

太郎：いえ、とっくに別れちゃいましたよ。ていうか、一緒にいる彼、超かっこよくないですか？　紹介してくださいよ。

まさし：そうしてあげたいけど、今、時間がないのよ。また今度ね。

太郎：ええ!?　残念。じゃあせめて、名前だけでも。……はじめまして。太郎です。

マーク：こんにちは。マークです。

太郎：日本にお住まいなんですか？

マーク：いえ、ニューヨークに住んでいます。今、旅行で日本に来ているんです。

太郎：いつまでいらっしゃるんですか？　良かったら連絡先を教えてください。

まさし：ちょっとマーク、そろそろ移動するわよ！

オープンカフェ……歩道や広場など、屋外に設けられたカフェ。日本の都市部でもちらほら見られるが、厳しい道路事情が妨げとなっているのか、欧米ほど発達していない。

Dialog 6

Sister Masako!?

Daisuke: Masashi! Is that OK what you did to him, acting so brusquely?

Masashi: It's OK. That kid may move quick, but he's also quick to lose interest——he lacks self-discipline, in other words. It's better for Mark to stay away from him.

Daisuke: Wow, you sure do get around, don't you? You even have acquaintances among guys who have a fetish for foreigners.

Miho: What do you mean by that? "Even ... guys who have a fetish for foreigners."

Daisuke: The Japanese gay world is broken down into unique communities representing people's different preferences——even drinking establishments and events——so it's unusual to meet people outside one's sphere.

Miho: Even though they're all gay, everyone is so different!

Mark: By the way, Taro just called Masashi "Masako-**né-san**" (**Sister** Masako) a bit back.

Daisuke: In Japanese, female first names often end in "ko." So here in Japan, gays sometimes use female-sounding names on purpose when addressing each other.

Mark: Same as in the States.

Masashi: Wait, Daiko! You didn't need to explain all that to him!

"né-san" (sister)   Originally a term of respect used for a woman older than oneself, gays use it sometimes even when calling someone younger than themselves. In that case, though, the nuance is that the younger person is even more queenie, or less innocent, than oneself.

まさ子ネエさん!?

「ゲイの世界は、好みのタイプ別に細分化されている」と、美穂に説明する大輔。
一方マークは、まさしが「まさ子ネエさん」と呼ばれていたのが、疑問の様子。

大輔：まさしさん、いいんですか？ あんなに素っ気ない対応をして。
まさし：いいのよ。あの子、手は早いし、飽きるのも早いし、根性悪いの。あんなのには近づかない方が、マークのためよ。
大輔：それにしてもまさしさんって本当に顔が広いんですね。外専の子にまで知り合いがいるなんて。
美穂：「外専の子にまで」ってどういうこと？
大輔：お店もイベントも、好みのタイプ別に細分化されていて、独自のコミュニティができあがっているから、タイプが違う人とは、なかなか知り合う機会がないんだ。
美穂：一口に「ゲイ」といっても、みんな違うのね……。
マーク：ところでさっき、太郎さんがまさしさんのことを「まさ子ネエさん★」って呼んでいましたね。
大輔：「●子」というのは、女性の名前の最後に、よく付けられる言葉なんだ。日本では、ゲイ同士が、相手をわざと女性的な名前で呼ぶことがあるんだよ。
マーク：それはアメリカも同じです。
まさし：ちょっと大子！ そんなことまで説明しなくていいわよ！

ネエさん……もともとは、年上の女性に対する尊称のようなものだが、ゲイ同士の場合は、年上が年下に呼びかける時に使うこともある。ただしその際、「自分よりおネエ度が高い」「自分よりスレている」などの意味がこめられていることもある。

Dialog 7
What's an "SG-kei"?

Mark: This place is quite big!

Masashi: Yes, this is "Kusuo" (meaning "Kyushu Otoko," or guys form Kyushu.) It sometimes hosts big events and even provides a practice space for square-dance teams. On weekends, the whole place is chaotic, with young people, old people, skinny people, "SG-**kei** (SG-**type**)," etc. Here's the owner, Mattchan.

Mattchan: Welcome, and enjoy your time here.

Mark: Thanks.

Miho: By the way, what's an "SG-kei"?

Daisuke: It's short for "super gattchiri," and refers to guys who are basically muscular, but tending to be overweight. Like those guys over there, for example. Can you spot them? The big-bodied guys with short hair and beards, wearing rugby shirts. Those are typical SG types.

Masashi: Recently, several other terms have also come to be used for well-built guys who are fat, such as "gachipocha."

"kei" (type)　There are all sorts of names for different "types" of gays : nerd-like guys who might easily be found in Akihabara (an electronics town) are called "Akiba-kei," while those who might be engaged in physical labor are called "gaten-kei." Those who like wearing loose-fitting fashion in a hip-hop style are called "B-kei." The term "kuma-kei" refers to large guys who are as hairy as "kuma" (bears).

SG系って何？

次にまさしが3人を連れて行ったのは、かつてフレディ・マーキュリーも訪れたことがあるという、仲通り沿いの「九州男」。その広さに驚くマークたち。

マーク：このお店はずいぶん広いですね。
まさし：ここ「九州男(くすお)」は、イベント会場として使われることもあるし、スクエアダンスチームの練習場所にもなっているの。週末には、若いのやら年配やら、細いのやらSG系★やら、とにかくいろんな人が集まって、カオス状態よ。こちらがオーナーのまっちゃん。
まっちゃん：いらっしゃい。ゆっくりしていってね。
マーク：ありがとうございます。
美穂：ところで、「SG系」って、何？
大輔：「スーパー・ガッチリ」の略で、筋肉の上に脂肪が乗った体型のことなんだ。たとえばほら、あの人たち。身体が大きくて短髪で、髭生やしてラガーシャツ着てる。彼らが典型的なSG系かな。
まさし：最近では、体格はいいけど脂肪分が多い人を指す「がちぽちゃ」とか、いろいろな言葉が出来ているのよね。

系……秋葉原にいそうなオタクっぽい人を「アキバ系」、肉体労働者風の人を「ガテン系」、ヒップホップ風のルーズなファッションの人を「B系」などといったりもする。なお「熊系」は、熊のように大柄な体型で、体毛の濃い人。

Dialog 8

Japanese gays are lenient toward fat guys.

Miho: Are "gachipocha" popular, too?
Daisuke: Yeah, a lot of gays like guys with flabby bodies.
Masashi: It's not just a matter of liking flabby types. For a long time now there have been **"debu-sen"** (chubby fetish). Surprisingly a lot of them are cute, as well.
Mark: Really? Japanese gays are lenient toward fat guys, it seems.
Daisuke: I've often heard people tell me that when they were skinny, no one used to pay any attention to them, but once they put on some extra weight, they suddenly gained in popularity. Maybe everyone feels a sense of ease around chubby guys.
Miho: They call this era an "age of healing."
Daisuke: That's something a bit different, I think!
Masashi: Anyway, I hear that fat people who get hit on by chubby chasers aren't quite sure if they are being loved for themselves, or just for their fat.
Miho: Everyone has a different type of hang-up, it seems.

"debu-sen"   Short for "debu-senmon," indicating a preference for fat men ("debu"). Incidentally, gays who have a preference for plump ("pottchari-shita") men are called "pocha-sen," while those who like obese guys whose weight in kilograms can be expressed in three digits (i.e., 100kg or more) are called a "mike-sen" (literally, "three-digit" fetish). In contrast, those who like skinny types are called "gari-sen."

日本のゲイは、脂肪に寛容なんですね……

体型談義に華が咲く4人。「日本人ゲイの間では、脂肪の多い身体も人気がある」と聞き、驚くマーク。

美穂：「がちぽちゃ」もやっぱり人気なの？

大輔：ゆるめな体型が好きな人は多いよね。

まさし：ゆるめが好きどころか、**デブ専**★の子も、昔からいるしね。しかも意外と、かわいい子が多いのよね。

マーク：そうなんですか？ 日本のゲイは、脂肪に寛容なんですね……。

大輔：「やせてる時は全然もてなかったのに、肉がついたとたん、急にもてるようになった」という話も、よく聞くよ。みんな、ぽっちゃりした体型に安心感を覚えるのかな。

美穂：今、「癒しの時代」って言われてるものね。

大輔：それとはちょっと違う気が……。

まさし：でも、デブ専の子にモテる人って、自分が愛されているのか、自分の肉が愛されているのか、わからなくなるらしいわよ。

美穂：人それぞれ、いろんな悩みがあるんですね……。

デブ専……「デブ専門」の略で、太目の人が好きな人のこと。ちなみに、ぽっちゃりした人が好きな人を「ぽちゃ専」、体重が三桁の人が好きな人を「ミケ専」、逆に、やせた人が好きな人を「ガリ専」という。

Dialog 9

I've been constantly dumped the past few years.

Miho: The gay world sure runs deeper than I thought, what with people's preferences being broken down by age and body type and all that.

Masashi: And that's not the end of the story, by any means. There's also the "okami" (wolf) fetish for slim but hairy types, and the "kuma" (bear) fetish for fat hairy guys, and the "single-edged eyelid" fetish for guys whose eyes look like that (found often in northern Asians), and the "ugly" fetish for homely guys, and the "suits" fetish for guys who wear suits, and the "mama" fetish for "mama-san" bar managers. There's even a **"dare-sen" ("anybody OK") fetish** for guys who will sleep with anyone!

Miho: It's hard to keep up, understanding all those categories. But it seems there is something for everybody.

Daisuke: There's even a saying, "There's no garbage to be dumped in Ni-chome."

Masashi: Well, I've been constantly dumped the past few years.

Daisuke: Hey, don't get so depressed all of a sudden like that. Shouldn't we be going to "akta" pretty soon?

Masashi: Before we do that, though, there's somewhere else I want to show you first.

"dare-sen" (anybody OK) fetish   Used for a gay who can fall in love or have sex with any type of guy. Also includes for those whose preference is not settled yet, or for those whose preference ends up being for the type of the person they happen to fall for. The term "erabu-dare-sen" has recently come to be used, which contradictorily means "picky dare-sen," for those who are basically not picky about something like age or body type, but choosy about some specifics like facial looks or hairstyle ("erabu" means "choose").

アタシはここ何年も捨てられっぱなしよ

ゲイの「好みのタイプ」の細かさに驚く美穂に、「二丁目に捨てるゴミなし」という言葉を教える大輔。それを聞いて、何故かまさしは落ち込む。

美穂：年齢や体型によって、そこまで好みのタイプが細分化されているなんて……。ゲイの世界って、奥が深い……。

まさし：あら、それだけじゃないわよ。他にも、やせてて毛深い人が好きな狼専、太ってて毛深い人が好きな熊専、一重まぶたの人が好きな一重専、不細工な人が好きなブス専、スーツを着た人が好きなスーツ専、ゲイバーのママが好きなママ専なんてのもあるんだから。中には、**誰専**★って人もいるけどね。

美穂：そこまでいくと、わけがわかりませんね……。でもみんな、どこかのカテゴリーにはひっかかりそう。

大輔：「二丁目に捨てるゴミなし」ということわざもあるくらいだからね。

まさし：アタシは、ここ何年も捨てられっぱなしよ……。

大輔：そんな、急に落ち込まないでくださいよ……。そろそろ「akta」へ行きませんか？

まさし：その前に、ちょっと見せておきたいところがあるの。

誰専……「どんな男とも恋愛やHができるゲイ」のことだが、「特にタイプが決まっていない人」「好きになった人がタイプ、という人」も含む。また「年齢や体型はどうでもいいが、顔にはこだわる」といった人もおり、彼らは「選ぶ誰専」といわれている。

Dialog 10

The buildings are left from the old red-light district days.

Mark: The buildings in this area look all smushed together. I wonder how many bars are crammed into this narrow space.

Miho: The entrance to each one is so small! But there's a real nostalgic atmosphere to the alleyway——a "good ol' days" kind of feeling.

Masashi: This is **Shin-Chidori-gai**. Some buildings are left from the old red-light district days.

Miho: Oh, really?

Masashi: When I think that there used to be women working here, it gives me a sentimental sort of feeling.

Miho: But it's quite amazing that these buildings have stood the test of time over all these years.

Masashi: There seems to be a tangle of land and building property rights involved. Even during the bubble years (of the late 1980s), the land sharks couldn't lay hands on them.

Daisuke: I see. An earthquake or fire would do the buildings in, but I do hope they last.

Shin-Chidori-gai Originally there was a "Chidori-gai" to the rear of Shinjuku Gyo-en, but street-widening efforts forced a land readjustment, moving the block to Ni-chome in 1967 ("shin" means "new"). More than four decades have elapsed since the move, but the block retains its atmosphere from then.

赤線時代の建物が今も残っているの

「九州男」のすぐ近くの路地へ、3人を案内するまさし。
そこは「新千鳥街」といって、赤線時代の建物が、今も残っているという。

マーク：ずいぶんごちゃごちゃしたところですね。この一角に、一体何軒のお店が入っているのかな。

美穂：一軒一軒の間口も狭い……。でもすごく趣があるというか、懐かしい感じがする路地ですね。

まさし：ここは「**新千鳥街**★」。赤線時代の建物が今も残っているの。

美穂：ええ!? そうなんですか?

まさし：ここで女たちが働いていたと思うと、何かしみじみした気持ちになるのよね……。

美穂：それにしても、よくこんな建物が残っていますね。

まさし：土地と建物の権利関係が複雑になっているみたい。だから、バブル期の地上げにも合わなかったらしいわ。

大輔：なるほど……。地震とか火事があったら大変そうだけど、こういう建物は残っていてほしいな。

新千鳥街……もともとは新宿御苑の裏手にあった「千鳥街」が、道路拡張に伴う区画整理により、1967年に二丁目に移転。以後約40年が経過した今でも、当時の姿を残している。

Column 3

芸能人と二丁目
Celebrities and Ni-chome

「ゲイバー街」という性質上、客のプライバシーが守られやすいということもあって、新宿二丁目には昔から、ゲイ・ノンケ、洋の東西を問わず、さまざまな芸能人が訪れています。イギリスのロックバンド「QUEEN」のボーカリスト、故フレディ・マーキュリーが、日本公演の度に「九州男」を訪れ、「I'm back!」(帰ってきたよ!)と叫んだというエピソードは、今も二丁目の伝説として語り継がれています。また最近、日本のスター歌手・倖田來未が、「club ArcH」のイベントでゲリラライブを行い、話題となりました。

一方、二丁目界隈に店を出す芸能関係者も、少なくありません。1952年にデビューし、ゲイであることをカミングアウトし、今も歌手・俳優・タレントとして活躍中の美輪明宏も、1970年代後半、二丁目の近くで「巴里」というクラブを経営していたそうです。

Owing to its nature as a gay bar area, where customers' privacy is tightly maintained, Shinjuku Ni-chome has long been popular among celebrities both gay and straight, and both Eastern and Western. When the late Freddie Mercury (1946-91) of the British rock band "Queen" visited "Kusuo" on the occasion of his band's performance in Japan, he shouted out, "I'm back!" That episode is now legendary in Ni-chome. Also, more recently, the Japanese star singer Kumi Koda (1982-) caused a considerable stir by giving a "guerilla" live performance at an event held at "club ArcH."
Meanwhile, quite a few celebrities have opened their own establishments in the Ni-chome vicinity. The club "Paris" is said to have been run in the late 1970s near Ni-chome by the singer, actor, and entertainer Akihiro Miwa (1935-), who made his/her debut in 1952, coming out later as gay.

Scene 4
Ni-chome as an information center

二丁目の、情報ステーション

Dialog 1

This street is called "Lily Path."

Masashi: This street is called "Lily Path."
Mark: That's quite a pretty name. Where did it come from?
Masashi: Well, you see ... there are several **lesbian bars** here. And lesbians were sometimes called the "lily tribe" in Japan.
Mark: Is there a lot of interaction in Japan between lesbians and gays?
Masashi: Depends on who you talk to. Some lesbians and gays are real chummy with each other, while others have nothing at all to do with each other.
Daisuke: Since lesbians like women and gays like men, the type of bar they like and the places they have fun in are different, too. Despite being so close, there is surprisingly little common ground between the two.
Masashi: Still, you could probably say that friendships between lesbians and gays last longer, because the two groups don't compete in the arena of love, right? That's because their friendship won't rupture on account of fighting for the same person. They don't have to worry about their friendship being snatched away on account of romantic relationships.
Daisuke: Masashi, you make it sound like something happened to you in the past, right?
Masashi: A lot of different things did! Anyway, let's go upstairs!

---

lesbian bars Some do not let any men in, even if they are gay, while others allow men in with lesbian escorts. Others let any man in. The pricing at lesbian bars is a little bit more expensive than at gay bars, with drinks at shot bars generally costing around 700 yen.

「百合の小道」と呼ばれているの

「akta」の前の細い通りに立つ4人。
「百合の小道」の通りの名の由来を説明するまさし。

まさし：この通りは、「百合の小道」と呼ばれているの。
マーク：ずいぶんきれいな名前ですね。何故そんな名前が？
まさし：それはね……。このあたりに、**レズビアンバー**★が何軒かあるから。日本じゃレズビアンは「百合族」って呼ばれたりしているのよ。
マーク：日本は、レズビアンとゲイの交流は盛んなんですか？
まさし：人によるわね。親友みたいに仲良くしているレズビアンとゲイもいれば、全く交流のない人たちもいるし。
大輔：レズビアンは女性が好きで、ゲイは男性が好きだから、飲む店も遊ぶ場所も違ってくるしね。近いようで、意外と接点がなかったりするんだ。
まさし：でも、レズビアンとゲイって、恋愛相手がかぶらない分、友情は長続きしそうよね？ 同じ相手を取り合って友情が決裂するってことがないから……。色恋の前には、友情もへったくれもないからね……。
大輔：まさしさん、過去に何かあったんですか？
まさし：いろいろね……。さあ、上にいきましょ！

レズビアンバー……ゲイであっても、男性は絶対に入れない店もあれば、レズビアンに連れられてきた男性ならOKという店、完全に男性OKな店もある。ゲイバーより少し高めな店もあるが、ショットバー形式なら、一杯700円前後から。

Dialog 2

Here we are at "akta."

Masashi: Here we are at "akta." Oh, I see you're back, Ken'ichi!

Ken'ichi: Hi, Masashi.

Masashi: I brought some of my friends along with me. This is Mark, from America.

Ken'ichi: Nice to meet you. I hope you will have a pleasant visit here.

Daisuke: It's friendly and relaxing here. Is this a community center or something?

Ken'ichi: Yes. It's set up by the Ministry of Health, Labour and Welfare through the **Japanese Foundation for AIDS Prevention**. It's a place to get information about HIV/AIDS, and also serves as a place for learning, information exchange, and interaction among people in the community.

Daisuke: Is it all right just to come here, without any specific purpose in mind?

Ken'ichi: We'll give you a big welcome. Use it as a rendezvous place for your friends, and other things. You can find magazines and drinks here, too.

Miho: There seems to be something on display back there.

Ken'ichi: Today we're exhibiting pictures from last year's Parade. Occasionally we also put on other events here, as well as language courses and sign-language classes.

Japanese Foundation for AIDS Prevention An organization set up in June 1987 with the purpose of spreading correct knowledge and sharing information about HIV/AIDS. Also works for the diagnosis and treatment of the disease, and enhancement of the system to prevent it. The management of "akta" has been entrusted to "RAINBOW RING."

「akta」に到着

「akta」に到着し、健一に声をかけるまさし。
健一は4人に、「akta」がどのようなスペースなのかを説明する。

まさし：ここが「akta」よ。……ああ、健一、戻ってるわね。

健一：まさしさん、こんにちは。

まさし：今日は友だちを連れてきたの。こちらは、アメリカから来たマーク。

健一：はじめまして。ゆっくりしていってくださいね。

大輔：明るくて落ち着きますね。ここは、コミュニティセンターなんですか？

健一：はい。厚生労働省が**エイズ予防財団**★を通じて事業化したもので、HIV/AIDSに関する情報提供等を行う場、コミュニティの人たちの学習・情報交換・交流の場として作られたものなんです。

大輔：特に用事がなくても、来ちゃっていいんですか？

健一：大歓迎です。友だちとの待ち合わせなんかにも使ってください。雑誌や飲み物もありますよ。

美穂：奥で、何か展示してますね。

健一：今日は、去年のパレードの写真を展示しています。時々ここで、イベントを行ったり、語学講座や手話教室を開いたりしているんですよ。

エイズ予防財団……HIV/AIDSについての正しい知識の普及啓発や情報交換、診断・治療・予防体制の充実などを目的として、1987年6月に設立された財団法人。なお「akta」の運営は、「RAINBOW RING」に委託されている。

Dialog 3

That's the ultimate form of safe sex!

Mark : What are these materials here?

Ken'ichi : They're flyers for various club events, documents describing STDs (sexually transmitted diseases), and booklets with the voices of HIV-positive people, and so forth.

Mark : Are there more and more HIV-positive people among Japanese gays, too?

Ken'ichi : Unfortunately, yes. The numbers are increasing every year. As of the end of 2007, a **total of 5,724 people** had gotten infected by HIV or come down with AIDS in Japan. And that is hardly the whole picture, it is said.

Mark : That's quite serious.

Masashi : Several educational and awareness groups have tried to distribute condoms and brochures, as well as organize events, but it's still an uphill task.

Daisuke : The information doesn't really reach gays who don't go to bars or participate in events, or who don't belong to specific activity circles.

Masashi : There are also quite a few guys who still want to do risky sex. I really wonder why people don't take better care of themselves. As for myself, I take such good care of myself that I haven't had sex the past few

---

total of 5,724 people   These numbers have been reported by the AIDS Surveillance Committee of the Ministry of Health, Labour and Welfare, and include cases through heterosexual contact. The same report also shows a total of 13,842 HIV-positive people and AIDS patients in Japan as of the end of 2007, 5,063 of whom came about through heterosexual contact.

それは、究極のセーフセックスですね

「akta」に置いてあるフライヤーやパンフレットに興味を示すマーク。
それをきっかけに、日本のゲイとHIV/AIDSについて話す大輔たち。

マーク：ここに置いてあるのは何ですか？

健一：クラブイベントのフライヤーや、性感染症に関する資料、HIV感染者の声を伝える冊子などです。気になるものがあったら、是非持って行って下さい。

マーク：日本のゲイの間でも、HIV感染者は増えているんですか？

健一：残念ながら、そうですね。年々増加傾向にあって、2007年末時点で、同性間の性的接触によるHIV感染者数およびエイズ患者数は、**5,724人**★という報告が出ています。しかしそれは全体の一部にすぎないとも言われています。

マーク：それは、深刻な状況ですね。

まさし：いろんな啓発団体がコンドームやパンフレットを配ったり、イベントをやったりしているんだけど、なかなかね……。

大輔：バーやイベントに遊びに行ったり、サークルに入ったりしていないゲイの人には、なかなか情報が行き渡りませんよね。

まさし：リスキーなセックスをしたがる人も、少なからずいるみたいだし……。どうしてみんな、もっと自分を大事にしないのかしら。アタシなんか、自分を大事にしすぎて、ここ何年もセックスしてないわよ！

大輔：それは、究極のセーフセックスですね……。

5,724人……厚生労働省のエイズ動向委員会報告によるもので、異性とも性的接触をした人を含む。なお同報告によると、2007年時点で判明しているHIV感染者およびエイズ患者の総数は13,842人で、異性間のみの性的接触によるHIV感染者およびエイズ患者の総数は5,063人。

Dialog 4

Don't treat it like somebody else's problem!

Masashi: Hey, Miho! Don't treat it like somebody else's problem! The number of people infected through heterosexual contact has been climbing, too.

Miho: Is that so?

Masashi: It's a big mistake to think of condoms as simply a contraceptive device. "**Safer sex**" means making fully sure your partner wears his condom all the time, even on your "safe days"!

Miho: OK, I understand. But first, I'll need to find a partner.

Masashi: You, too, are a pathetic woman! By the way, Ken'ichi, excuse my abrupt question, but have you ever lived in Boston?

Ken'ichi: Nope, I've lived in Tokyo my whole life.

Masashi: Oh, I see. Oh, and tell me, are you seeing someone now?

Ken'ichi: Yes. It's been around a year, exactly, since we started going together, I think.

Masashi: You cute guys are popular, just as I expected! Thanks for telling me all these things.

Ken'ichi: No problem. Come back here again!

Safer sex   Refers to being careful not to be infected by any infectious disease, including HIV, during sex, and includes the wearing of condoms and not swallowing sperm. The term "safe sex," meanwhile, means having no sexual intercourse at all, but just engaging in mutual masturbation, etc.

他人事みたいな顔しないのっ!

まさしは美穂にも、セーファーセックスを心がけるよう注意する。
そこから強引に、話題を、「健一の身元調査」にもっていくまさし。

まさし：ちょっと、美穂! 他人ごとみたいな顔して聞いてんじゃないわよ! 男女間でのセックスによる感染者だって、増えているんだから。

美穂：そうなんですか?

まさし：コンドームを避妊のためだけの道具だと思ったら大間違い。安全日でも、ちゃんと相手につけさせるのが**セーファーセックス★**よ!

美穂：はい、わかりました……。でも、その前にまず、相手を探さないと。

まさし：アンタも淋しい女よね……。ところで、つかぬことをきくけど、健一って、ボストンに住んだこと、ある?

健一：いえ、生まれてから今まで、ずっと東京ですよ。

まさし：そう……。ちなみに今、彼氏はいるの?

健一：はい。つきあいはじめて、ちょうど1年くらいかな。

まさし：かわいい子は、やっぱり売れるのね……。いろいろと教えてくれてありがとう。

健一：いえいえ。また遊びに来てくださいね。

セーファーセックス……「コンドームを使用する」「精液を飲み込まない」など、HIVを含むあらゆる感染症に感染しないよう注意して行うセックスのこと。なお「セーフセックス」は、マスターベーションの見せあいなど、完全にセーフなセックスのこと。

Dialog 5

That's what's known as a gay shop.

Masashi: That's too bad (Ken'ichi wasn't Yohei), Mark.
Mark: Yeah. Well, maybe I'll run into the real Yohei in the future!
Masashi: You sure got over that fast!
Mark: By the way, what's that shop over there? I've been curious about it for a while now.
Masashi: Oh, you mean "LUMIERE"? That's what's known as a gay shop. It sells gay-related books, magazines, DVDs, underwear, adult toys, etc. There must be stores like it in New York, too, right?
Mark: Yes. But I'd like to see a Japanese gay magazine.
Masashi: So let's go in then.
Miho: Can I go too?
Masashi: It's all right, as long as you stay near the entrance. I seem to remember that women are prohibited from going to the DVD corner, though.
Daisuke: Or maybe the two of us should wait outside together again?
Miho: Yes, that might be better. Thanks.
Masashi: Don't get mistaken for a "**Lumiko**!"

Lumiko Someone who waits in front of "LUMIERE" scouting out guys or waiting to be hit on. People who wait in front of the rice shop kitty-courner across from "LUMIERE" are known as "Yoneko," while those who wait in Shinjuku Park are called "kimiko."

ここはいわゆるゲイショップよ

再び仲通りへと戻った4人。
そこでマークが、ゲイショップ「ルミエール」に興味を示す。

まさし：残念だったわね、マーク。
マーク：はい……。でもこれから、本物のヨウヘイくんに会えるかもしれませんから！
まさし：立ち直り早いわね……。
マーク：ところで、さっきからずっと気になっていたんですが、あのお店は？
まさし：ああ、「ルミエール」ね。ここはいわゆるゲイショップよ。ゲイ関連の書籍や雑誌、ゲイDVD、下着、大人のおもちゃなんかを売ってるの。こういうお店、ニューヨークにもあるでしょ？
マーク：はい。でも、日本のゲイ雑誌、見てみたいですね。
まさし：じゃあ、中へ入りましょうか。
美穂：私も入って大丈夫？
まさし：入り口付近までは大丈夫じゃないかしら。DVDコーナーは、女性は立ち入り禁止だったと思うけど。
大輔：それともまた、一緒に外で待っていようか？
美穂：うん、その方がいいかも。ありがとう。
まさし：「**ルミ子★**」と間違えられないようにね！

ルミ子……「ルミエール」の前に立って、男を物色したり、声をかけられるのを待っていたりする人。なお、「ルミエール」の斜め前の米屋の前に立つ人を「米子」、新宿公園に立つ人を「公子」という。

Dialog 6

They're smaller and thicker than American gay magazines.

Masashi : These are Japanese gay magazines lined up here.
Mark : They're smaller and thicker than American gay magazines.
Masashi : There used to be some large-sized magazines published, too, but the only ones left are all this size.
Mark : There are several types of magazines——how does their content differ?
Masashi : As you might expect, the magazines are divided by type. "Badi" is mainly for those who like younger guys, while "G-men" is a magazine for those who like more solid, masculine-looking types. The term "SG type" was invented by this magazine.
Mark : I see. How about this magazine, then?
Masashi : It's "SAMSON," for guys who are chubby chasers. The magazines "Himawari" and "She-male" are for guys who like to cross-dress. Incidentally, these are back-numbered issues of "anise" and "Carmilla" ——both are lesbian magazines that have discontinued publication.
Mark : By the way, what's this slightly strange-looking magazine in a book format?
Masashi : It's "Queer Japan Returns," a book edited by **Noriaki Fushimi**. It's quite informative!

Noriaki Fushimi (1963-) A novelist and commentator. In 1991, he published "Private Gay Life," in which he came out as a gay. The book had a big impact on the gay movement in Japan. His book, "Majo no Musuko" ("Son of a Witch") won the 40th Bungei-sho Award in 2003, and marked his debut as a novelist.

アメリカのゲイ雑誌より小さくて厚いですね

「ルミエール」店内にて。日本のゲイ雑誌のサイズや厚さに、驚くマーク。
まさしは、各雑誌の特徴について、細かく説明する。

まさし：ここに並んでいるのが、日本のゲイ雑誌よ。

マーク：アメリカのゲイ雑誌より小さくて厚いですね。

まさし：大きなサイズのゲイ雑誌も何度か発刊されたんだけど、今残っているのは、結局全部このサイズなのよね。

マーク：何種類かありますが、内容はどう違うんですか？

まさし：雑誌もやっぱり、タイプ別に分かれているの。『Badi』は主に、若い子が好きな人向けの雑誌。『G-men』はガッチリした、見た目が男っぽいタイプが好きな人向けの雑誌ね。「SG系」という言葉は、この雑誌から生まれたものなの。

マーク：なるほど。この雑誌は？

まさし：『サムソン』は、デブ専の人向けの雑誌よ。で、『ひまわり』とか『シーメール白書』は、女装を楽しむ人向けの雑誌ね。ちなみにこの『anise』と『Carmilla』は、レズビアン向けの雑誌のバックナンバー。今は休刊になっているわ。

マーク：ところで、このちょっと変わった判型の雑誌は？

まさし：『Queer Japan Returns』ね。**伏見憲明★**さんが編集した本で、ためになるわよ！

伏見憲明……小説家、評論家。1991年に『プライベート・ゲイ・ライフ』を出版し、ゲイであることをカミングアウト。ゲイ・ムーブメントに大きな影響を与えた。また2003年に『魔女の息子』で第40回文藝賞を受賞し、小説家としてもデビューした。

Dialog 7

Look at how many gay DVDs there are!

Masashi : From here all the way to the back is the gay DVD corner!

Mark : Look at how many there are! These are DVDs featuring SG types, right?

Masashi : Right. And here are some with younger guys in them.

Mark : Oh! The model in this DVD is so cute!

Masashi : Wanna buy it? Or maybe you'd rather take a look at the used DVD shop called "CONVOY," which is close to here.

Mark : I wonder if can I play Japanese DVDs in the States? In that case I'll just get a copy of a gay magazine while I'm here.

Masashi : And how about some **underwear**? There are a lot of different designs, like those that make your crotch look bigger.

Mark : No, that's all right. ... By the way, what are all these things displayed here?

Masashi : Those are molded candies. If you buy something at this store, you can get one for free.

---

underwear Although many gays have been interested in underwear for many years, the low-rise boxer sold by the men's underwear brand, TOOT, launched in 2001, has become especially popular among them. Thereafter, several new brands of men's underwear have appeared on the scene, with a lot of shops springing up in Ni-chome selling underwear exclusively, such as "BALZAAL."

ゲイDVD、ものすごくたくさんありますね

若い子が出てくるDVDを気に入った様子のマーク。
しかし結局、ゲイ雑誌だけを買うことに。

まさし：ここから先が、ゲイDVDのコーナーよ！

マーク：ものすごくたくさんありますね。これはSG系のDVDですね。

まさし：そう。若い子が出てくるのは、この辺ね。

マーク：あ！　このDVDのモデルの子、かわいいですね……。

まさし：買ってく？　それとも近くに「コンボイ」って中古DVDショップがあるから、何ならそこに行く？

マーク：日本製のDVDって、アメリカでも観られるのかな？
とりあえずゲイ雑誌だけ1冊買っていきます。

まさし：あと、**下着**★は？　股間が大きく見えるデザインのやつとか、いろいろあるわよ。

マーク：いや、そこまでは結構です。……ところで、ここにたくさん並んでいるのは何ですか？

まさし：駄菓子よ。このお店で買い物をすると、駄菓子がおまけでついてくるのよ。

下着……以前から、下着にこだわるゲイは少なからずいたが、2001年に立ち上げられた男性下着ブランド「TOOT」のローライズボクサーが、ゲイの間で大人気に。以後、新しい男性下着ブランドも続々登場し、二丁目にも「バルザール」などの下着専門店ができている。

Dialog 8

There's an "O-né" celebrity!

Masashi: Sorry to make you guys wait! ...Hey, Daisuke, Miho! Isn't that person over there one of the "O-né" (queenie) celebrities appearing in "O-né, MANS!"?

Daisuke: You're right! That's the first time I've seen one in the flesh.

Mark: What's "O-né, MANS!"?

Masashi: It's a TV variety show starring just queenie celebrities. They also have other professional jobs, though, such as an acclaimed hair stylist or a flower arranger.

Mark: Really? Japan has shows like that, too?

Miho: There are even some trendy Japanese phrases made popular by such celebrities.

Mark: Such as what?

Daisuke, Masashi, Miho: **"Don dake——!"**

Mark: What does that mean?

Daisuke: How should I explain it ... something like "how far (are you gone)?," maybe.

Masashi: Perhaps it's impossible to explain in English.

"Don dake——!" A phrase used when making a comeback after a comment or joke. Became a candidate for the 2007 Buzzwords-of-the-Year Contest after the hair-stylist IKKO (1962-) popularized it after it was introduced as a phrase popular among members of the LGBT brass band, "Brass MIX!," which had made an appearance in a variety show.

おネエタレントを目撃!

「ルミエール」前で、まさしは、テレビのバラエティ番組に出てくる
おネエタレントを目撃。ここ数年の、おネエタレントの活躍ぶりが話題に。

まさし：お待たせ！ ……ちょっと大輔、美穂！ あそこにいるの、「おネエ・MANS!」に出てるおネエタレントじゃない？

大輔：本当だ！ 初めてナマで見た。

マーク：「おネエ・MANS!」って何ですか？

まさし：ヘアメイクとか華道家とか、他に仕事を持ちながら、おネエタレントとしても活動している人ばかりを集めた、テレビのバラエティ番組よ。

マーク：へえ。日本にも、そんな番組があるんですね。

美穂：おネエタレントの方が広めた流行語もありますよね。

マーク：どんな流行語なんですか？

大輔・まさし・美穂：どんだけー !★

マーク：それはどういう意味ですか？

大輔：何て説明したらいいんだろう……。How far、とかかなあ。

まさし：英語で説明するのは不可能なんじゃないかしら。

どんだけー !……ツッコミを入れる際に使われる言葉。バラエティ番組に出演したLGBT のブラスバンド「Brass MIX!」が、「団内の流行り言葉」として紹介したものをヘアメイクアーティストのIKKOが広め、2007年の流行語大賞候補ともなった。

Dialog 9

"Fujoshi" have become a hot topic of conversation.

Daisuke: The **Kohaku Uta-gassen** (literally, "Red-White Song Match") in 2007 was quite something. There were a lot of people who didn't fit into standard gender definitions, such as queenie celebrities and a transgender singer-songwriter, Ataru Nakamura (1985-). They even said, "We belong to the Pink Team!"

Miho: Recently, "fujoshi" (rotten girls) have become a hot topic of conversation.

Mark: "Fujoshi"?

Masashi: It means "rotten girls." In other words, girls who are fixated on reading novels or comics that depict love stories between two men, or who fantasize about characters from comics as well as pop idols having homosexual sex.

Daisuke: I heard that some of them even try to get their boyfriends to have sex with other men.

Mark: What a complicated situation! You don't find such a culture in the United States.

Masashi: I think I'm getting a little tired. How about if we go have some tea somewhere?

Kohaku Uta-gassen (Red-White Song Competition) First aired by the Japanese public television network NHK in 1951, the competition takes place every New Year's Eve, and is broadcast live. Several dozen famous singers are divided into the "red group" (women) and the "white group" (men), and they compete with their songs and performances. The audience rating for the show is exceedingly high, so much so that at one time it was called a "monster program."

「腐女子」も話題よ

仲通りを歩きながら、2007年の紅白歌合戦や、「腐女子」について語る4人。
しかしマークには、「腐女子」という存在がよくわからない様子。

大輔：2007年の**紅白歌合戦**★もすごかったね。おネエタレントとか、トランスジェンダーのシンガーソングライターの中村中とか、男女の枠に入りきらない人が、たくさん出ていて。しかも「私たちは桃組です！」なんて言ってたし。

美穂：最近は、「腐女子」も、話題になっていますよね。

マーク：腐女子？

まさし：「腐った女子」という意味よ。男の子同士の恋愛を描いた小説や漫画にハマってたり、漫画のキャラクターやアイドルなどが「もし男性同士で恋愛していたら……」と妄想したりする女性のことなの。

大輔：中には、自分の恋人の男性に、男性と恋愛させようとする女性もいるらしいよ。

マーク：それはとても複雑ですね……。アメリカにはない文化です。

まさし：ところでアタシ、ちょっと疲れちゃった。お茶でもしない？

紅白歌合戦……NHK（日本の公共放送）で、1951年から毎年大晦日に放送されている、生放送の大型歌番組。数十組の歌手が、紅組（女性）と白組（男性）に分かれて、歌や演奏を競い合う。視聴率が非常に高く、「お化け番組」といわれていた時期もある。

Dialog 10

So it's sort of an information center for Ni-chome as well.

Mark : This place seems almost full. We're lucky we got in!
Masashi : "CoCoLo cafe" is the perfect place to take a break from bar-hopping and having fun at events. It's always crowded on weekends.
Miho : Even so, it has a nice, relaxing atmosphere.
Masashi : The use of indirect lighting and candles is great. It makes facial imperfections harder to see as well!
Mark : Would it be OK if I had something to eat? I'm starving!
Masashi : Of course. If you really want to satisfy your hunger, you ought to order the "CoCoLo Plate" or the "Season Plate." They're both filling, and the menu changes every week or every season. I love them both.
Miho : They also have a good selection of drinks and desserts. I feel like a kid in a candy store here!
Mark : By the way, what are all those photos on the wall?
Masashi : Every month, this place has **exhibits of artworks** by different artists, such as photos or paintings or illustrations.
Mark : So it's sort of an information center for Ni-chome as well.

---

exhibits of artworks With quite a lot of gays involved in artistic and expressive activities, several establishments in Shinjuku Ni-chome and San-chome, among other places, exhibit their artwork. A group exhibition is also held every summer by a group of LGBT artists called "rainbow arts."

ここも、二丁目の情報センターなんですね

「ココロカフェ」に入って、一息入れる4人。
美穂は、店の雰囲気とメニューの豊富さが気に入った様子。

マーク：ほぼ満席ですね。入れて良かった！
まさし：「ココロカフェ」は飲み歩いたりイベントで遊んだりしている途中で、一息つくのに、ちょうどいいお店なのよね。週末はいつも混むのよ。
美穂：でも落ち着いた、いい雰囲気ですね。
まさし：間接照明やキャンドルを使っているのが、いいのよね。顔のアラも見えにくくなるし……。
マーク：何か食べてもいいですか？　お腹が空いてしまって。
まさし：もちろん。しっかり食べたいなら、「ココロプレート」か「季節のプレート」がおススメよ。ボリュームもあるし、週ごとか季節ごとに内容が変わるし、アタシ大好きなの。
美穂：ドリンクやデザートの種類も豊富なのね。目移りしちゃう。
マーク：ところで、壁にたくさん写真が貼ってありますね。
まさし：このお店は月替わりで、写真とか絵画とかイラストとか、いろいろなアーティストの**作品を展示**★しているのよ。
マーク：ここも、二丁目の情報センターなんですね。

作品展示……ゲイの中には、何らかの表現活動をしている者が少なくなく、二丁目や三丁目には、作品の展示を行っている店がいくつかある。また、LGBTのアーティストが集まったグループ「rainbow arts」は、毎年夏にグループ展を開催している。

ゲイブームと二丁目
The "gay boom" and Ni-chome

1991年、女性誌『CREA』が「ゲイ・ルネッサンス'91」と題した特集を組んだのをきっかけに、レズビアンやゲイを扱った書籍や雑誌記事、テレビ番組、映画などが急増しました。「ゲイブーム」と呼ばれたこの現象により、世間の「ゲイ」に対する認知度が急速に高まり、新宿二丁目を訪れる人も増加。それまで「同性愛者たちの出会いの場」として、どちらかといえば閉ざされた状態にあった二丁目は、この時期を境に、徐々にオープンになっていったのでした。

また1993年には、連続ドラマ「同窓会」が放送され、同性愛を大きく扱った内容が話題に。ドラマ中のゲイバーは、二丁目に実在する店をモデルとして作られ、二丁目でのロケも実施されました。以来、二丁目は、しばしばテレビドラマやバラエティ番組、雑誌記事等に登場することとなりました。

Since 1991, when the women's magazine "CREA" published a feature on "Gay Renaissance '91," there has been a sharp spike in the number of books, magazine articles, TV shows and movies dealing with lesbians and gays. This phenomenon was described as a "gay boom," and drastically increased the popular awareness of gays among the Japanese general public, pushing up the number of people visiting Shinjuku Ni-chome as well. Before then, Ni-chome was rather a closed place devoted solely to gays getting to meet each other, but it gradually became more open after that time. Also, the serial drama "Doso-kai" (Reunion) was broadcast in 1993, spotlighting homosexuality in a big way. The gay bar appearing in the drama was modeled after a real one in Ni-chome, and some shots were even made on location in Ni-chome. Thereafter, Ni-chome has frequently come to appear in TV dramas and variety shows, as well as magazine articles.

Scene 5
Various facts about Ni-chome you wanted to know

もっと知りたい、いろんな二丁目

Dialog 1

Ni-chome is really a scary place, so full of temptations!

Miho: Are there any other places that serve food in Ni-chome besides the "CoCoLo cafe?"

Masashi: Yes. Even just along Naka-dori, you can find **soba noodle shops**, sushi bars, ramen noodle shops, Chinese porridge shops, and even an Italian restaurant, mostly run by straight people, some for decades.

Daisuke: The number of lesbian-run and gay-run pub-like restaurants and bars serving food has also grown recently.

Masashi: When I get hungry after drinking, I often go to such places.

Daisuke: That's why you've gained a little extra weight!

Masashi: Oh, shut your mouth! I can't help overeating because the food tastes so good. It's the fault of the restaurants!

Daisuke: What nonsense!

Masashi: There are also stalls selling delicious "takoyaki" (fried octopus balls). I can't stop myself from buying a pack when I catch a whiff. Ni-chome is really a scary place, so full of temptations!

---

soba noodle shop For some unknown reason, Ni-chome has a lot of soba noodle shops. At one time, there were seven such places competing with each other for customers. Some of them stay open until dawn, and are frequented by many gays.

二丁目は誘惑だらけの恐ろしい街……

「ココロカフェ」に満足した様子のマークたち。
美穂から質問され、二丁目の食事どころについて答える大輔とまさし。

美穂:二丁目には「ココロカフェ」以外にも、食事ができるお店はあるんですか？

まさし:あるわよ。仲通り沿いだけでも、ノンケの人が昔からやってるお**蕎麦屋**★さんやおすし屋さん、ラーメン屋さん、中華粥屋さん、あと、イタリアンレストランなんかもあるわね。

大輔:レズビアンやゲイの人がやってる居酒屋風のお店とか、食事のできるバーも、最近増えてますよね。

まさし:飲んでてお腹が空いた時に、アタシもよく行くわ。

大輔:そんなことしてるから、贅肉が……。

まさし:うるさい！ 美味しいから、つい食べ過ぎちゃうのよ！ お店のせいよ！

大輔:そんなめちゃくちゃな……。

まさし:屋台の美味しいたこ焼き屋さんもあるしね。あの匂いを嗅ぐとアタシ、ついつい1パック買ってしまうのよ。二丁目ってほんと、誘惑だらけの恐ろしい街だわ……。

蕎麦屋……二丁目には何故か蕎麦屋が多く、一時は7軒ほどの店がしのぎを削っていた。明け方まで営業している店も何軒かあり、多くのゲイに利用されている。

Dialog 2

That toilet is a "hattenba."

Mark: By the way, is that a park there?
Daisuke: Yeah, it's called Shinjuku Park.
Miho: There are a lot of people there. What are they all doing?
Masashi: Some are gay friends who are just talking with each other, while others are cruising for a trick, and some want people to pay for sex. Incidentally, that public restroom is a **"hattenba" (cruising spot)**.
Mark: I see.
Miho: Hmm, it doesn't seem to be a place for a woman to be in at nighttime. I'd just get in everyone's way.
Masashi: Still, during the daytime on weekends, you'll see a lot of families here on outings. A lot of homeless people also loiter here as well.
Daisuke: Sometimes you'll find gays performing music here, too.
Masashi: Anyway, it has to be a really generous park to take in so many different kinds of people and things!

"hattenba" (cruising spot) A place where gays go to find a sexual partner. Some "hattenba" are businesses that require a fee to get in, such as saunas and video boxes (places to watch adult videos in private rooms), while others are freely accessible, such as parks, public toilets, and movie houses.

そのトイレはハッテン場よ

「ココロカフェ」の斜め前にある公園に気づき、興味を示すマーク。
まさしは「時間帯によって変わる、公園のさまざまな表情」を語って聞かせる。

マーク：ところで、そこにあるのは公園ですか？
大輔：うん。新宿公園というんだ。
美穂：たくさん人がいるわね。みんな、何をしているの？
まさし：ゲイの友だち同士がおしゃべりしてたり、出会いを求める人がいたり、お金をもらってHする人を探していたり。ちなみにそのトイレは、**ハッテン場★**よ。
マーク：なるほど。
美穂：じゃあ、夜は女子は近づかない方がいいわね。みなさんの邪魔になるから……。
まさし：でも、休日の昼間には、家族連れがここで遊んでいたりするのよ。ホームレスの人も、結構いるけどね。
大輔：時々、ここで音楽を演奏しているゲイもいますよね。
まさし：とにかく、いろんな人やものを飲み込んでいる、懐の大きな公園ってことよ。

ハッテン場……Hの相手を求めるゲイが集まる場所。サウナやビデオボックスなど、店舗営業をしている有料のハッテン場もあれば、公園や公衆トイレ、映画館などを、ゲイが勝手に利用していることもある。

Dialog 3

What do mean by "new half" and "onabe"?

Masashi : So, Let me take you to several places that are a bit different (from the ones we went to already). Anyway, let me take you to a **"new half" show pub bar** I know well, though I'd really like to show you an **"onabe" bar** too, if I could.

Mark : What do you mean by "new half" and "onabe?"

Daisuke : In Japan, "new half" refers to men dressed up as women, or those who are formerly men, who work at bars and the like. Some of them have actually had sex-change operations, while others are cross-dressers while remaining physically male.

Mark : So they're different from transgendered people and transvestites?

Daisuke : Hmm, there are some things they have similar and/or in common, but it's not completely the same concept.

Masashi : Anyway, the types of bars where such people wait on customers or put on shows are called "new half" In contrast, "onabe" bars are the reverse of "new half" show pub bars, in that their staff are women dressed up as men, or women who have undergone a sex change.

Mark : I see. Japan sure has a lot of different types of gay establishments!

"new half" show pub bars, "onabe" bars Not so common in Ni-chome at all, but rather more often found in other areas of Tokyo such as Kabuki-cho (also in Shinjuku). Most of the clientele are straight. Charging around 4,000 yen, they cost more than ordinary gay bars to get in, as the fee includes a charge for watching a show performed.

ニューハーフとかおなべって、何ですか?

「これから何件か、ちょっと変わったお店に連れて行く」と宣言するまさし。
手始めに、まずはニューハーフショーパブに行くことに。

まさし:さて、これから何軒か、ちょっと変わったお店に連れて行くわね。**おなべバー★**も捨てがたいけど、とりあえず、アタシがよく知ってる**ニューハーフショーパブ★**に行くわよ!

マーク:ニューハーフとかおなべって、何ですか?

大輔:日本では「女性の格好をして、バーなどで働いている男性や元男性」をニューハーフと呼んでいるんだ。性転換手術を受けた人もいれば、身体は男性のままで、女装だけしている人もいるけどね。

マーク:トランスジェンダーとかトランスヴェスタイトとは違うんですか?

大輔:うーん、似た部分や共通している部分はあるけど、完全に同じ概念というわけではないかな。

まさし:でね、彼女たちが接客をしたり、ショーを見せたりするのが、ニューハーフショーパブなの。おなべバーは、ニューハーフショーパブとは逆に、男性の格好をした女性や元女性が働いているお店のことよ。

マーク:なるほど。日本にも、いろいろなお店があるんですね。

ニューハーフショーパブ、おなべバー……いずれも二丁目にも数軒あるが、歌舞伎町や六本木など他の地域で営業している店も多い。ショーチャージが入るため、料金は 4000 円程度からと、一般のゲイバーよりは高め。

Dialog 4

What do gays think about straights who visit Ni-chome.

Masashi: This is the "new half" show pub bar, "La SAISON." It's the first time for you, too, Daisuke, isn't it?

Daisuke: Yes.

Masashi: Actually not so many gays go to show pubs or **"kanko"(tourist) bars**.

Mark: A "Kanko"(tourist) bar.

A Masashi: It's a bar for straight guys and girls who want to get a taste of the gay world. It's probably safest for straights who know nothing about gays or Ni-chome to visit such a bar. I think it's enjoyable for them.

Miho: What do gays think about straights who visit Ni-chome?

Masashi: Everyone has his own idea or the matter. Those gays who can only feel relaxed when drinking at a Ni-chome bar with other gays resent having straights come in, while those who want to make friends with a lot of people, no matter what their sexuality is, probably get a kick out of it. At any rate, no one likes the kind of straight person who storms into a gay bar and acts as if he owns the place. ...Oh, the show seems ready to begin. Watch the stage now.

"kanko" (tourist) bar A gay bar mainly targeting a straight clientele that wants to enjoy conversing with the gay "mama" and staff. A little bit more expensive than bars targeted at gays. Some of these establishments have separate price settings for gays and straights.

二丁目に来るノンケをどう思っているんですか？

ニューハーフショーパブ「ラ・セゾン」に着いた4人。
美穂はまさしに、ある質問をする。

まさし：ここがニューハーフショーパブ「ラ・セゾン」よ！　大輔も初めてでしょ？

大輔：そうですね。

まさし：ショーパブとか**観光バー**★に行くゲイの子って意外と少ないのよ。

マーク：観光バー？

まさし：「ゲイの世界をのぞいてみたい」という、ノンケ男女向けのバーよ。ゲイや二丁目のことをよく知らないノンケは、とりあえずショーパブとか観光バーに行った方が無難だし、楽しめるんじゃないかしら。

美穂：ゲイの人たちは二丁目に来るノンケをどう思っているんですか？

まさし：人それぞれよね。「二丁目のバーでしかリラックスして飲めない」というゲイは、ノンケが来るのを嫌がるだろうし、「セクシュアリティなんて関係なく、いろんな人と友達になりたい」と思っているゲイは、ノンケが来ることも面白がるだろうし。ただ、ゲイ向けのバーで、我が物顔で騒いじゃうノンケは、いずれにせよ嫌がられるわね。……あら、そろそろショーが始まるみたい。ステージに注目よ。

観光バー……主に、ゲイのママや従業員との会話を楽しみにくるノンケ男女をターゲットとしたゲイバー。料金は、ゲイ向けのバーに比べて、若干高め。ゲイ料金とは別に、ノンケ料金が設定されている店もある。

Dialog 5

Well, if it isn't the "busu" one!

Masashi: Hey, Miho, you look transfixed.

Miho: It's just that the show was so great.... The dancing was beautiful, and the things they said were funny. ...Oh! Isn't that one of the dancers coming here?

Reiko: I'm Reiko. Welcome. Well, if it isn't the **"busu"** (**ugly**) one!

Miho: Ugly ... is she talking about me? What the nerve, saying something like that out of the blue!

Masashi: Wrong, it's me she's referring to. But in this town, it's not a bad thing to be called "ugly." It shouldn't seriously be taken as meaning "ugly looks."

Reiko: Well, in your case, I really did mean to say you're ugly! And these three people, is it your first time to visit my bar?

Daisuke, Miho, Mark: Y- yes.

Reiko: My, such a cutie! Anyway, have a good time before leaving. Also, I need to have a word with you!

Miho: With me?

Reiko: Just because you're pretty, don't let it get to your head! Anyway, I have a bigger breast than you. Granted, it isn't real....

Miho: Uh, I, I see!

"busu" (ugly)   Originally meaning someone who has a bad face (or personality). But some gays like to use this phrase when calling out to each other, such as "'Busu,' good morning!" and "You're really a 'busu'!" But these are really expressions of affection, and have nothing to do with whether someone really has a good (or bad) face or personality.

あら、ブス、いらっしゃい!

ニューハーフショーパブ「ラ・セゾン」店内にて。
大輔と美穂、そしてマークは、ショーガール・レイコの激しい接客にたじろぐ。

まさし:ちょっと美穂、何ボーっとしてるのよ。
美穂:ショーが凄く素敵で…。踊りはきれいだし、トークは面白いし。…あ! さっき踊ってたお姉さんが!
レイコ:レイコです。いらっしゃいませ。やだ、**ブス★**じゃない!
美穂:ブスって……私のこと? そんな、いきなり……。
まさし:違うわよ、アタシのこと。でも、この街で「ブス」って言われるのは、悪いことじゃないのよ。別に、本気で「不細工」って言われてるわけじゃないんだから。
レイコ:あら、アタシ、アンタに対しては、本気でブスって言ったつもりなんだけど。こちらの3人は、ウチの店は初めて?
大輔・美穂・マーク:は、はい。
レイコ:まあ、かわいい。楽しんで行ってちょうだいね。それからアンタ!
美穂:私ですか?
レイコ:ちょっときれいだからって、いい気になっちゃダメよ。胸だってほら、アタシの方が大きいんだから! 作り物だけど。
美穂:わ、わかりました!

ブス……本来は顔(あるいは性格)が良くない人、という意味。しかしゲイの仲間同士の間では、「ブス、おはよう!」「アンタってほんと、ブスよね」といった具合に使われることが多い。これは親愛の情を示しているのであり、顔や性格の良し悪しとは無関係。

Dialog 6

Let's go to an "uri-sen" bar next!

Daisuke: Wow, that Reiko was sure aggressive!

Miho: But it was still a lot of fun!

Masashi: That's good. Well, let's go to an **"uri-sen" (money-boy)** bar "ANDERSEN" next!

Miho: What does "uri-sen" mean? Is it like "fuke-sen" (daddy fetish) or "debu-sen" (chubby fetish) or something?

Masashi: No, no! "Uri-sen" just means guys who exclusively "sell" themselves (for sex). Something like a host (at a host club), in other words. But it's different from the host clubs that you find in Kabuki-cho and elsewhere. It's a place where money is exchanged for sex. This is a good chance for Mark to get to talk with a cute Japanese boy.

Daisuke: Is it OK for Miho to tag along?

Masashi: That might be a bit difficult. A few "uri-sen" places do let girls in, though.

Miho: Don't bother about it! It's late already, so I better go home pretty soon.

Daisuke: Sorry, Miho. I'll send you a text message later.

Miho: Sure. See ya tomorrow, everybody!

"uri-sen" (money boy)   In some places featuring "uri-sen," customers can sit down with the boys and drink and talk, just as in regular gay bars. Some "uri-sen" establishments also have private rooms and offer dispatch (escort) services.

じゃあ今度は、売り専のお店に行くわよ!

「今度は売り専の店に行く」というまさし。
「売り専」の意味がわからない美穂に、その内容を詳しく説明する。

大輔:レイコさん、アグレッシブな営業だった……。
美穂:でも、すごく楽しかった。
まさし:あら、良かった。じゃあ次は、**売り専**★のお店「アンデルセン」に行くわよ!
美穂:売り専って何ですか? 老け専とかデブ専みたいなもの?
まさし:違う違う! 売り専は、売り専門……。要するに、ホストよ。といっても、歌舞伎町なんかのホストクラブとは違うわよ。お金をもらってHする場所、といったらいいのかしら。せっかくだからマークを、日本のかわいい男の子とお話させてあげたいじゃない。
大輔:美穂が行っても大丈夫かな?
まさし:ちょっとむずかしいかも。中には女性OKな売り専のお店もあるけど……。
美穂:気にしないで! もう遅いし、私そろそろ帰らないと。
大輔:美穂、ごめんね。後でメールするよ。
美穂:了解。また明日ね。

売り専……売り専の店には、普通のゲイバーのように、客とボーイとが酒を飲みつつ話すスペースを備えた店と、個室・出張専門の店がある。

Dialog 7

This is the kind of place where it pays to have fun!

Masashi : So, Mark, how do you like it? Your first money-boy place.

Mark : The boys are all cute, that's for sure.... But it makes me nervous to see them all lined up like that inside the counter.

Masashi : If any of them captures your fancy, just speak up and **point him out**. I'll get the manager to set you up with him. But remember, the only thing that will happen here is sitting down and talking with the boy. If you feel like it, you can come back here yourself alone!

Mark : Well, I don't think I'll get that that far....

Masashi : Don't be silly. This is the kind of place where it pays to have fun! It'll be your loss if you don't just give free rein to your own desires!

Daisuke : Masashi, you sure seem at home here.

Masashi : Duh——that's because I used to work here!

Daisuke : What! You've got to be kidding!

Masashi : Hey! Maybe you're thinking there's no one who'd buy me?!

Daisuke : Wh ... what are you talking about? I meant no such thing!

---

point him out In "uri-sen" places with bars, the customer first chooses the boy he wants to be with, and if he likes the boy after talking with him a little, they can go out together (to have sex) (some places have even set up private rooms for that purpose). The fee is around 1,300 yen or more for one drink (fees for sex are extra).

こういうところは楽しんだもんがちよ!

売り専の店「アンデルセン」を訪れた3人。
カウンターの中に並んだボーイたちを前に、緊張気味のマーク。

まさし:マーク、どうかしら？　初めての売り専は。

マーク:ボーイさんたち、みんなかわいいですね……。でも、カウンターの中にズラッと並ばれると、ちょっと緊張します。

まさし:気に入った子がいたら言ってね。マネージャーを通して、**指名**★するから。ただしここでは、飲みながらお話するだけね。もしその気になったら、後で一人で来てちょうだい！

マーク:いえ、そこまでは……。

まさし:何言ってんの。こういうところは楽しんだもんがちよ！　欲望の赴くままにガンガンいかないと、損よ！

大輔:まさしさん、すごく慣れてますね。

まさし:だってアタシ、昔この店で働いていたんだもの。

大輔:え！　本当ですか？

まさし:アンタ……。「売れっこない」とか思ったでしょ。

大輔:な、何言ってるんですか！　そんなことないですよ！

指名……バーを備えた店では、客はまず希望のボーイを指名して話をし、気に入れば一緒に外出する（個室を備えている店もある）。チャージ＋1ドリンク1300円程度から。

Dialog 8

Ryo is a "cho-ikemen."

Ryo : Nice to meet you, I'm Ryo. Thanks for choosing me.
Masashi : You're Ryo, I see. You're a "cho-**ikemen**" (super **good-looking guy**)! This is Mark, the guy who selected you.
Ryo : Hi. You're really good-looking!
Mark : Thanks.
Masashi : C'mon, Mark, you chose him, so at least hold hands with him!
Mark : Sure.
Masashi : Yes, yes, like that.
Daisuke : How old are you, Ryo?
Ryo : I just turned 21.
Masashi : My God! 21? That's why your skin is so smooth!
Ryo : Ha-ha ... thanks.
Daisuke : Hey, Masashi, stop taking advantage of the confusion, touching his body like that! You're getting carried away!

"ikemen" (**good-looking guy**) Comes from a combination of "ikete-iru" (meaning good-looking) and "men," which can either mean "face" in Japanese or the English word "men." In other words, it means a good-looking guy. The person who invented the phrase is an editor at the women's magazine "egg," first using it in the January 1999 issue.

リョウくんって超イケメン

「アンデルセン」店内にて。マークが指名した21歳のボーイ・リョウが、
大輔たちの席にやってくる。一人ではしゃぎまくるまさし。

リョウ：はじめまして、リョウです。ご指名ありがとうございます。
まさし：リョウくんね。超**イケメン**★！ こちらがあなたを指名したマークよ。
リョウ：こんにちは。すごくかっこいい方ですね。
マーク：ありがとう。
まさし：ほら、マーク、アンタが指名したんだから、手ぐらい握りなさい！
マーク：はい……。
まさし：そうそう、それでいいのよ。
大輔：リョウくんはいくつなんですか？
リョウ：この間、21歳になりました。
まさし：きゃー！ 21歳？ どおりでお肌なんか、ツルッツルだと思った！
リョウ：ははは……。ありがとうございます。
大輔：ちょっとまさしさん、何、どさくさにまぎれて、身体触ってるんですか！ はしゃぎすぎですよ！

イケメン……「かっこいい」を意味する「イケてる」と、「男」を意味するメンズ（あるいは「顔」を意味する「面」）の合成語で、「美男子」を指す現代用語。女の子向けの雑誌『egg』の編集者が考え出し、同誌の1999年1月号に初めて登場した。

Dialog 9

How about if we go to a "fundoshi" bar?

Masashi : Oh, Mark, you're so boring! You finally get the kind of guy you like to sit down next to you, and all you do is just hold his hands!

Daisuke : Can't be helped. I was there, too, and then there's the language barrier. In general, Mark is shy, not like you, Masashi.

Masashi : What do you mean by that? Even I was shy when I was your age. A dozen years have changed me....

Daisuke : Oh, is that it?

Masashi : Well, anyway, it's getting late. What are you guys going to do?

Daisuke : Maybe we ought to go home. Tomorrow's the Parade, after all.

Mark : Right.

Masashi : Aw, c'mon! You're just going to go quietly home like that? How about if we go to a **"fundoshi" (loincloth) bar**? Or maybe a "hattenba" (cruising spot)? I'll lead you as far as their entrances!

Mark : A "fundoshi" bar and a "hattenba?"

Daisuke : Masashi, what in the world is it that you're trying to get Mark to do?!

"fundoshi" (loincloth) bar   Although more often found in places like Asakusa, "fundoshi" (loincloth) bars and SM bars also exist in Ni-chome as well. The customers don't always have to put on loincloths, however——usually, there are special "fundoshi" days for that.

ふんどしバーもあるわよ

何事もなく、「アンデルセン」をあとにした4人。
「そろそろ帰る」というマークを、もっと遊びなさいと煽るまさし。

まさし：もう、マークつまんなーい！ せっかくタイプの子が席に着いたのに、手を握るだけなんだもん。

大輔：仕方ないよ。僕も一緒だったし、言葉の問題もあるし。大体、マークはまさしさんと違って、シャイなんだから。

まさし：何よアンタ。アタシだって、アンタくらいの歳の頃はシャイだったわよ。十数年の年月が、アタシを変えたのよ……。

大輔：そうでしたか……。

まさし：ところで、だいぶいい時間になったけど、アンタたちはどうする？

大輔：そろそろ帰ろうか？ 明日はパレードだし。

マーク：そうですね。

まさし：やだ！ おとなしく帰る気？ **ふんどしバー★**にでも行けば？ それともハッテン場がいい？ お店の前までは案内するわよ！

マーク：ふんどしバーに、ハッテン場ですか……？

大輔：まさしさん、一体マークに何をさせたいんですか……。

ふんどしバー……浅草等に比べると軒数は少ないが、二丁目にも、ふんどしバーやSMバーなどがある。ただし、ふんどしバーとはいっても、客が全員、いつもふんどしをつけているわけではなく、ふんどしデーなどが別に設けられていることが多い。

Dialog 10

Can foreigner go to "hattenba" in Ni-chome, too?

Masashi: I want Mark to get a good taste of Japanese gay culture, from one corner to the other! It's parental love! Besides, we might find Yohei there.

Daisuke: Wrong! think he actually would not enjoy running into his first boyfriend at a "hattenba" (cruising spot)!

Masashi: Well, it seems that while we've been talking, we've already reached "24 Kaikan." This is a sauna for gays and is also a "hattenba" (cruising spot). It has a big bath, and a "mix room," too. Also, there are several video-box cruising spots in this vicinity. You'll probably find more **"Johnny-style" guys** (young, cute pop-idol type boys) there.

Daisuke: Masashi, can foreigners (westerners) go to cruising spots in Ni-chome, too?

Masashi: Not every place lets them in. I think you'll find more foreigners in cruising spots around Akasaka.

Daisuke: You sure are an expert on it! Anyway, let's call it a day and go home.

Mark: That seems to be the best thing to do.

"Johnny-style" guys   Refers to young, cute guys, who would feel right at home in the major talent agency, Johnny & Associates, to which a lot of popular male idols belong. The type of gay who has a fetish for such boys is called a "Johnny-sen."

二丁目のハッテン場は外国人も入れるの?

まさしについて歩いているうちに、サウナ系ハッテン場「24会館」の前に
やってきた大輔たち。しかし結局、中には入らず、解散することに。

まさし:アタシはねえ、マークに、日本のゲイカルチャーを隅から
隅まで、しっかり味わってほしいのよ! 親心よ! それに、
もしかしたらヨウヘイくんがいるかもしれないじゃない。

大輔:いや、ハッテン場で初恋の人に会うのは、かえって嫌だと思
うよ。

まさし:とか何とか言っているうちに、「24会館(にいよん)」に着いちゃった。
ここはサウナ系のハッテン場よ。大きなお風呂や、ミックス
ルームがあるの。あと、この界隈には、ビデオボックス系の
ハッテン場も、何軒かあるわよ。**ジャニ系★**は、そっちの方
が多いかも。

大輔:でもまさしさん、二丁目のハッテン場って、外国人も入れる
んですか?

まさし:入れないところもあるわよ。それから、赤坂あたりのハッ
テン場にも、外国人がよく来てるわね。

大輔:詳しいですね……。でも、とりあえず今日は帰ろうよ。

マーク:その方が良さそうですね……。

ジャニ系……男性アイドルが多数所属している「ジャニーズ事務所」にいそうな、若くて
かわいい男の子のこと。ジャニ系が好きな人のことを「ジャニ専」という。

Column 5

インターネットと二丁目
The Internet and Ni-chome

インターネットや携帯電話の普及で、ゲイたちの出会いや交流の幅が、飛躍的に拡大しました。中でも、日本最大級のシェアを誇るソーシャル・ネットワーキング・サービス（SNS）「mixi」に、ゲイはいち早く反応。ゲイ専用のコミュニティ（共通の趣味や考えを持つメンバーが集う掲示板）も数多く作られました。またゲイ専用の出会い系サイトや、「HUGS」「Men's mixjp」といったゲイ専用のSNS、さらには多言語対応の、グローバルなゲイ専用SNSなども登場しています。

このようにネット社会化が進むと、「ゲイの出会いの街としての新宿二丁目が衰退するのではないか」と危ぶむ声もあります。しかし一方で、店のサイトを立ち上げたり、SNS上にその店のコミュニティを作ったりするなど、ネットを宣伝や新規客の獲得に利用する店も増えています。

Thanks to the spread of the Internet and mobile (cell) phones, the opportunity for gays to meet one another and date has increased dramatically. One of Japan's largest social networking services (SNSs), "mixi," has particularly been well-utilized by gays from early on, with many special communities (bulletin boards for members with common hobbies and ideas) created especially for gays. There are also dating websites especially for gays, as well as gay-exclusive SNSs such as "HUGS" and "Men's mixjp," along with multilingual global gay-only SNSs.

On account of the development of the Internet society, some people have feared that the role of Shinjuku Ni-chome might decline as an area for gays to get together. On the other hand, there are an increasing number of establishments there that are utilizing the Net for advertising their business and gaining new customers, putting up their own websites and creating their own SNSs communities.

Scene 6
Joining the Tokyo Pride Parade

東京プライドパレードを、歩く

Dialog 1

Shall we go to Yoyogi Park now?

Daisuke: Is Masashi ever late! He said he would meet us at the Harajuku Station ticket gate at 10 o'clock.

Miho: Maybe it's taking him some time to get ready.

Daisuke: Probably. They say, "When waiting for fags to show up, you have to add an extra five minutes for each person before everyone will come." But in Masashi's case, it's more like 15 minutes!

Mark: Oh, a drag queen is coming closer. Could that be Masashi?

Masashi: Good morning! Sorry for being late. It took me a long time to apply my makeup, since I'm not used to doing it normally. Anyway, how about this outfit?

Mark: Looks great! It's sort of neo-futuristic.

Masashi: You see? I worked hard making it all through the night!

Daisuke: Did you really wear that on the train here?

Masashi: Sure! I wanted as many people to see me as possible.

Daisuke: So you've already done a one-person parade, I see!

Masashi: Come, shall we go to **Yoyogi Park** now?

Yoyogi Park A park in Shibuya Ward, Tokyo. Because it can hold so many people, and has an outdoor stage, the event plaza in Yoyogi Park has been used as the starting and ending point for LGBT parades in Tokyo since 1996.

さあ、代々木公園に移動するわよ!

東京プライドパレード当日、午前10時15分。
原宿駅改札前でまさしを待つ大輔たちの前に、一人のドラァグクイーンが現れる。

大輔:まさしさん、遅いなあ。10時に原宿駅の改札で、って言ったのに。

美穂:準備に時間がかかってるんじゃない?

大輔:たぶんね。「オカマが待ち合わせをすると、人数×5分後にやっと全員が揃う」って言うけど、まさしさん一人で15分遅れてるよ……。

マーク:あ……。ドラァグクイーンが一人、近づいてくる。もしかしてまさしさん?

まさし:おはよう! ごめんね、遅くなって。普段やり慣れないもんだから、メイクに時間かかっちゃった。どう? この衣装。

マーク:かっこいいですよ! 近未来風で。

まさし:でしょう? 夜なべして、頑張って作ったわよ!

大輔:でも、その格好で電車に乗って、ここまで来たんですか?

まさし:もちろん! できるだけ多くの人に見てもらいたいもの。

大輔:すでに、一人でパレードしてきたんですね……。

まさし:さあ、**代々木公園**★に移動するわよ!

代々木公園……東京都渋谷区にある公園。大人数を収容できること、野外ステージがあることなどから、1996年以降、代々木公園のイベント広場が、東京のLGBTパレードの出発・帰着地点となっている。

Dialog 2

Which float shall we walk with?

Masashi: So anyway, let's register.
Daisuke: People are already lined up at the registration!
Masashi: That's because the popular **floats** fill up fast. People who have their eye on a particular float start waiting around early.
Mark: For my information, tell me what kind of floats there are.
Daisuke: Some floats have brass bands, while there are others for the parade organizers, and some for club events for lesbians and gays. Every year there are floats themed on popular singers such as Seiko Matsuda (1962-) and Ayumi Hamasaki (1978-) —— female singers popular among Japanese gays. I wonder if we'll see them this year as well.
Mark: All of them seem so interesting. Which one shall we walk with?
Masashi: I plan to join the Shinjuku Ni-chome Promotion Association Float. Won't you go along?
Mark: Let's do that. I want to go with Masashi.
Masashi: My goodness, Mark, you do make me happy!

---

floats   The Tokyo Pride Parade features a dozen or so floats sponsored by corporations or groups. Participants in the Parade must register in advance the float that they want to walk behind. The maximum number of people behind each float is 200.

どのフロートと一緒に歩く？

代々木公園に到着した4人は、まず受付へ。
大輔、美穂、マークも、まさしと同じフロートの後ろを歩くことに。

まさし：とりあえず、受付をすませましょう。

大輔：もう、受付に並んでる人がいる！

まさし：人気のある**フロート**★は、すぐに定員に達しちゃうからね。お目当てのフロートがある人は、早い時間から待機してるのよね。

マーク：ちなみに、どんなフロートがあるんですか？

大輔：吹奏楽のグループのフロートもあれば、パレードの実行委員会のフロートとか、レズビアンやゲイのクラブイベントのフロートもあるよ。毎年、日本のゲイに人気のある松田聖子や浜崎あゆみといった歌手をテーマにしたフロートも出てるけど、今年はどうかな？

マーク：どれも面白そうですね。僕たちはどこに並びましょうか？

まさし：アタシは、「新宿二丁目振興会フロート」で歩くつもり。アンタたちも一緒に並ぶ？

マーク：そうしましょう。まさしさんと一緒に歩きたいです。

まさし：やだ、マーク、嬉しいこと言ってくれるじゃない。

フロート……東京プライドパレードには、企業や団体によるフロート（山車）が十数台出展される。パレード参加者は事前に、どのフロートの後ろを歩くか決めて、受付をすませなければならない。なお、1つのフロートの後ろを歩ける人数は、最大で200人まで。

Dialog 3

They're booths set up by the Parade's sponsors.

Mark: By the way, what are all these tents standing here?

Daisuke: They're **booths** set up by the Parade's sponsors, exhibiting various things.

Mark: Each of them is selling a lot of different things, like books and T-shirts.

Miho: There are also booths set up by publishers and movie distributors. Not all of them are gay-related corporations——some ordinary companies are also exhibiting.

Daisuke: There are also booths by HIV/AIDS awareness groups and non-profit organizations.

Masashi: This booth is giving out "uchiwa" fans. It's hot, so let's take some!

Daisuke: Masashi just loves to take anything he can get for free!

Masashi: What's that you said?!

Mark: There seem to be more stalls set up in the back.

Daisuke: Those are food stalls. I think they're selling things like "taco-rice" (taco filling placed on top of rice) and curry. Let's go have some later when we're hungry.

---

booths At the event site, various booths are set up by the Parade's sponsors, along with those selling official Parade goods, a space for a free market, tents for general information and for first-aid, stations to throw away garbage, and a booth by the Parade's planning committee.

パレードのスポンサーによる出展ブースだよ

受付をすませ、会場内を見て回る4人。
パレードスポンサーの出展ブースなどについて、マークに説明する大輔。

マーク：ところで、テントがたくさん並んでいますが、これは？
大輔：パレードのスポンサーによる出展**ブース**★だよ。
マーク：本とかTシャツとか、それぞれいろいろなものを売っているんですね。
美穂：出版社のブースや、映画の配給会社のブースもあるわ。ゲイ関係の企業だけでなく、一般企業も出展しているのね。
大輔：HIV/AIDSの啓発団体とか、NPO法人のブースもあるよ。
まさし：このブースではうちわを配っているみたい。暑いからもらっていきましょ！
大輔：まさしさん、タダでもらえるものに目がないんだから。
まさし：何ですって！
マーク：奥の方にも、お店が出ていますね。
大輔：あれは、食べ物の屋台だよ。タコライスとかカレーとかを売ってるんじゃないかな。後でお腹が空いたら、食べに行こう。

ブース……会場内には、スポンサーの出展ブースの他に、パレードの公式グッズ販売、フリーマーケットスペース、そして総合案内や救護テント、ゴミステーションなど、パレード実行委員会によるブースもある。

Dialog 4

Always ready with a comeback, you fag!

Masashi: A whole lot of people have turned out despite the bloody heat. Oh, if it isn't Takeko!

Takeshi: My God! Sister, it's been a while!

Masashi: My, look who's showing off a lot of skin! What theme did you pick this year, "sumo wrestler" or something?

Takeshi: It's you who has a lot of spunk, sister! What's your theme, "mermaid marooned on land?"

Masashi: Always ready with the comeback, you fag! But that's what I like about you!

Takeshi: Sorry, you're the only I can't keep up with.

Miho: What a war of words!

Daisuke: We'd better watch from a safe distance.

Mark: Hey! Something has started on stage.

Daisuke: It's the opening **stage event**.

Mark: Let's go watch. I don't understand the language, though.

Miho: What about Masashi?

Daisuke: As long as he's on the Parade site we can meet up later. Leave him be for now.

---

stage event   On the day of the Pride Parade, various events are held on the outdoor stage from morning until evening. They include symposia related to LGBT issues, performances by bands (see the next section), and the kick-off ceremony for the Parade, etc.

口の減らないオカマね

会場内でまさしは、おネエ友達のたけしに遭遇。
二人の激しい舌戦にとまどう大輔たち。その時、ステージイベントが始まり……。

まさし：しかしこのクソ暑いのに、よくこんなに人が集まるわね。……あら！ ちょっと、たけ子！

たけし：やだ！ ネエさん、久しぶり！

まさし：アンタ、すごい露出の多さね……。今年のテーマは何？ 幕下の力士？

たけし：ネエさんこそ、気合入ってるじゃない。テーマは陸に上がった半魚人？

まさし：相変わらず口の減らないオカマね、アンタって。でもそういうアンタが好きよ。

たけし：ごめんなさい。アタシ、ネエさんとだけはヤれないわ……。

美穂：すごい舌戦……。

大輔：遠巻きに眺めていようよ。

マーク：あ！ ステージで何か始まりましたよ。

大輔：**ステージイベント★**のオープニングだね。

マーク：行ってみましょう。言葉はよくわからないけど……。

美穂：まさしさんは？

大輔：会場内にいれば後で会うだろうし。放っていこう……。

ステージイベント……パレード当日、野外ステージでは午前中から夕方まで、イベントが行われている。内容は、LGBTに関するシンポジウムや、吹奏楽の合同演奏（次ページ参照）、パレードの出発セレモニーなど。

Dialog 5

The "Brass with Everybody!" event is about to start.

Mark: A lot of people with musical instruments have shown up on stage.

Daisuke: The "Brass with Everybody!" event is about to start.

Miho: There certainly are a lot of people. I wonder if they can all fit on stage.

Daisuke: According to the guidebook for the parade, there are more than 100 people participating. **People who can play musical instruments** have gathered from around the whole country, and they will put on a once-off performance without any rehearsal.

Mark: That sounds interesting.

Masashi: Hey, you all! Why did you leave me behind?

Daisuke: Oh, Masashi! Sorry about that! But let us know what you were up to until now.

Masashi: I was going around saying hello to everyone. It takes quite a while! That's because a lot of my acquaintances show up at well-attended events like this.

Daisuke: Are you OK? Your makeup is starting to run!

Masashi: Oh, no! I have to go redo it somewhere!

---

people who can play musical instruments As many LGBT people can play musical instruments, many have formed several bands and orchestras in various cities across the country, giving regular concerts. In recent years, those groups have stepped up their exchanges with each other, combining to give joint concerts, including the participation of LGBT choirs.

「"みんな"でブラス!」が始まるよ

引き続き、ステージ前にて。「"みんな"でブラス!」の演奏が始まるのを
待っている大輔たちのもとへ、まさしが戻ってくる。

マーク：今度は、楽器を持った人がたくさんステージ上に集まってきました。

大輔：これから、「"みんな"でブラス!」という企画が始まるんだ。

美穂：すごい人数ね。ステージ上におさまりきるのかしら。

大輔：パレード当日用のガイドブックによると、参加者は100人以上だって。全国から**楽器経験者**★が集まって、リハーサルなしの本番一発勝負で演奏するらしいよ。

マーク：それは面白そうですね。

まさし：ちょっとアンタたち！　よくもアタシを置いてけぼりにしたわね。

大輔：わー！　まさしさん、ごめんなさい！　ていうか、今まで何してたんですか？

まさし：挨拶回りよ……。こういう、人がたくさん集まるイベントにくると、知り合いが多くて大変なのよ……。

大輔：だ、大丈夫ですか？　すでにメイク、とけはじめてますよ。

まさし：大変！　どこかで直さなきゃ。

楽器経験者……楽器経験のあるLGBTは多く、全国にいくつかの吹奏楽団や弦楽合奏団があり、定期演奏会も行われている。さらに合唱団を含めた複数の音楽系サークルによる合同演奏会が開催されるなど、近年、楽団間の交流がいっそう活発になっている。

Dialog 6

The Parade is about to begin, finally!

Masashi : Oh, the Parade is about to begin, finally!
Daisuke : Masashi seems to have fixed up his makeup all right.
Masashi : Naturally, since the main event is about to begin!
Miho : I'm really excited——it's the first time for me to take part in a Japanese (Pride) Parade. Everyone seems to be having fun, just like in New York.
Daisuke : Right. Compared with the time I first participated, there seem to be more people taking part in everyday clothes. They don't even bother to cover their faces anymore, either.
Miho : That's because there's a lot more people who dare to take part openly.
Mark : The line has started to move. Oh, that scared me ... cars are passing right alongside the Parade!
Miho : That's understandable. During the gay parade in New York, the street is completely closed to traffic.
Masashi : That would be practically impossible here, given the road conditions in Tokyo. In the **Sapporo Parade**, though, the roads are a little wider. Anyway, it's dangerous, so be careful not to go outside of the marked lane!

Sapporo Parade Since 1996, an LGBT parade has been held practically every year in Sapporo, Hokkaido (its current name is "Rainbow March Sapporo"). Also, the Kansai Rainbow Parade began in 2006. LGBT groups have taken part in other local festivals in places like Kobe and Hakata.

さあ、いよいよパレード出発ね!

代々木公園のケヤキ並木に並び、出発を待つ4人。
辺りを見回し、思い思いの感想を述べ合う。

まさし：さあ、いよいよパレード出発ね！
大輔：まさしさん、メイク、バッチリ直してきましたね。
まさし：当たり前よ！　これからが本番なんだから！
美穂：日本のパレードに参加するのは初めてだから、ドキドキするなー。でもニューヨークと同じで、みんな楽しそう。
大輔：そうだね。それに、僕が初めて参加した時に比べて、普段着で参加している人が多い気がする。顔も隠していないし。
美穂：堂々と歩ける人が増えてきたってことなのね、きっと。
マーク：列が動き始めましたよ。……すぐ隣を、車が走っているんですね。びっくりしました。
美穂：ニューヨークのゲイパレードの時は、道路は完全に通行止めになるものね。
まさし：東京の道路事情では、なかなかそうはいかないのよ。**札幌のパレード**★では、もう少し道路を広く使えるんだけどね。危ないから、車線をはみださないように気をつけて！

札幌のパレード……札幌では 1996 年からほぼ毎年、パレード（現在の名称は「レインボーマーチ札幌」）が行われている。また、大阪では 2006 年から「関西レインボーパレード」が始まり、神戸や博多では、地域の祭りのパレードに、LGBT のグループが参加している。

Dialog 7

Somehow it really made me so happy.

Daisuke: It's boiling. Mark, are you OK? Here, have some water.

Mark: Thanks. That helps a bit. Anyway, it's real fun watching these performances on the floats.

Daisuke: They're **lip-synching** to songs by popular Japanese singers.

Mark: Also, it's a surprise to me that the people lining the streets are friendlier than I thought.

Masashi: A lot of them are gay like us, moreover. If you take a good look, you can see a lot of them carrying rainbow flags or the "uchiwa" fans handed out at the site.

Mark: You're right.

Masashi: I remember the first time I took part in one of these Parades. Even though all of us were just walking down the street like this, everybody seemed to be in it together——my friends with me, and the straight people waving at us from the side of the street. Somehow it really made me so happy.

Daisuke: Masashi, don't cry! You'll cause your makeup to run again!

---

lip-synching To move one's lips along with the words in a pre-recorded song, making it look like one is actually doing the singing. Also called "kuchi-paku" in Japanese. Shows that feature drag queens generally use lip-synching.

何だかとっても幸せな気持ち

パレードの最中、暑さにバテ気味なマークを気遣う大輔。
一方で、最初にパレードに参加した時のことを思い出し、感慨深げなまさし。

大輔：暑いけど、マーク、大丈夫？　この水、飲みなよ。

マーク：ありがとう。……少し楽になりました。しかし、フロート上のパフォーマンス、見ていて楽しいですね。

大輔：あれは、日本の人気歌手の曲に合わせて、**リップシンク★**をしているんだ。

マーク：それから、沿道の人が思ったよりフレンドリーで、驚きました。

まさし：あの中には、お仲間もいっぱいいるしね。よく見ると、レインボーフラッグとか、会場で配られていたうちわを持っていたりするでしょ。

マーク：本当だ。

まさし：最初にパレードに参加した時のことを思い出すわ……。ただこうやって道を歩いているだけなのに、一緒に歩いている友だちも、沿道で手を振ってくれるノンケの人たちも、みんな仲間なんだなあ、って、何だかとても幸せな気持ちになったのよね。

大輔：まさしさん、泣かないで！　またメイクが崩れますよ！

リップシンク……あらかじめ録音された、音声入りの楽曲に合わせて、歌っているように見せること。「口パク」と言われることもある。ドァグクイーンのショーは、リップシンクで行われることが多い。

Dialog 8

Are there any LGBT politicians in Japan who have come out?

Masashi : Gee, that was fun, but I'm exhausted! It's tough to walk for so long under the blazing sun, especially wearing this makeup and this outfit!

Daisuke : It's hard enough wearing regular clothes, so it must be that much worse for you, Masashi.

Mark : There's something beginning on the stage again.

Daisuke : It's the closing event.

Miho : I've seen that person on TV! Is he a politician?

Masashi : Lately, politicians have started to take part in the Tokyo Parade, and several political parties have come to deliver comments.

Mark : Are there any **LGBT politicians** in Japan who have come out?

Masashi : Sad to say, but no Diet member has come out as of yet, although we have some openly LG people who have run for the national legislature (without winning), such as Ken Togo (1932-) and Kanako Otsuji (1974-). However, there are some (local) politicians who have come out, such as Aya Kamikawa (1968-). She's a transgendered ward-councilwoman in Tokyo.

LGBT politicians   In the 2007 Setagaya Ward Council elections, Aya Kamikawa (1968-), an openly transgendered woman, won her second term. Several other politicians who have come out also ran in the nationwide local elections held the same year, although Kamikawa remains the only public elected official in the country.

カミングアウトした政治家はいるの？

パレード後のクロージングイベントで、コメントを述べる政治家たち。
それを見たマークが、大輔たちに、ある質問をする。

まさし：いやあ、楽しかったけど、疲れた……。炎天下で、メイクして衣装着て長時間歩くのはキツいわ……。

大輔：普段着で歩いているだけでも大変なのに、まさしさん、すごいですね。

マーク：またステージ上で何か始まりましたよ。

大輔：クロージングイベントだね。

美穂：あの人、テレビで見たことがある！ 政治家よね？

まさし：最近、東京のパレードにも、政治家が参加したり、各政党からのコメントが寄せられたりするようになったのよ。

マーク：日本には、カミングアウトしている**LGBTの政治家**★はいるんですか？

まさし：残念ながら、国会議員には今のところいないの。東郷健さんとか尾辻かな子さんとか、カミングアウトした上で国政選挙に挑戦した人はいるんだけどね。ただ、上川あやさんのように、東京都の区議会議員として頑張っている人はいるわ。

LGBTの政治家……2007年の東京都の世田谷区議会議員選挙で、性同一性障害であることをカミングアウトしている上川あやが、二期目の当選を果たした。同年の統一地方選挙では、他にも数名のLGBTが、カミングアウトして立候補している。

Dialog 9

Are they all volunteers?

Masashi : That's the last of the parade-related events.
Miho : Oh, the staff has begun to clean up. They've got to pull down everything ... the tables and the tents on the site. It must be hard, after having worked all day.
Mark : Are they all **volunteers**?
Masashi : Yes. Not just in this parade, but at all LGBT organizations and events. Without volunteers, none of them would ever get off the ground.
Daisuke : Maybe I'll volunteer next year.
Masashi : Oh, I'm impressed! By the way, what are you all going to do now? I'm bushed, so I think I'll go back home for now.
Miho : I'd like to call it a day, too. We started quite early this morning.
Daisuke : OK, Mark and I will have a bite to eat. Maybe we'll go to a gay bar in Shibuya.
Mark : Sounds great. Let's go!
Masashi : Don't overdo it now. We still have tomorrow to worry about!

---

volunteers The management of non-profit LGBT events depends entirely on the help of volunteers, as do most local gay-night events. Quite a few straight people also help as volunteer staff members.

彼らは全員、ボランティアなんですか?

クロージングイベント終了後、会場を片付けるボランティアスタッフに
目を留める美穂。大輔は、次回は自分もボランティアをしようと決意する。

まさし:これでパレード関連のイベントは一通り終わったわね。
美穂:あ……。スタッフの人たちが片付けを始めたわ。会場のテーブルやテント、全部片付けなきゃいけないのね。一日中働いた後なのに、大変そう。
マーク:彼らは全員、**ボランティア**★なんですか?
まさし:そう。このパレードに限らず、LGBTの団体やイベントって、ボランティアの人たちがいなければ、成り立たないものばかりなのよね……。
大輔:来年は僕も、ボランティアしようかな。
まさし:あら、偉いわね! ところでアンタたち、これからどうする? アタシは疲れたから、とりあえず一旦帰るわ。
美穂:私も、今日はここで。今朝早かったから。
大輔:じゃあ、マークと僕は軽く食事して……。渋谷のゲイバーに飲みに行く?
マーク:いいですね。行きましょう!
まさし:あまり無理しないようにね。明日もあるんだから!

ボランティアスタッフ……非営利のLGBTイベントの運営は、完全ボランティアで行われており、地方のゲイナイトなども、ボランティアスタッフによって支えられていることが多い。またボランティアスタッフの中には、異性愛者も少なくない。

Dialog 10

We've been together the whole time since last night.

Mark : This place is sure crowded!
Daisuke : Yeah. Especially today, right after the Parade.
Mark : About how many gay bars are there in **Shibuya**?
Daisuke : I'd say about eight. The past few years, there more gay bars have started to appear in Shibuya, especially those aimed at younger people.
Mark : I see. By the way, Daisuke, thank you so much for last night and today.
Daisuke : What's wrong? So formal all of a sudden.
Mark : These past two days have been really fun. Masashi treated me well, and you took care of me during today's Parade in a lot of ways. It made me happy.
Daisuke : Mark, this is your first Japanese summer, and I was worried whether you were OK after walking outside for so long.
Mark : It makes me sad to think we have to go our separate paths the day after tomorrow.
Daisuke : Right. We've been together the whole time since last night. Anyway, let's enjoy tomorrow's Rainbow Festival!

Shibuya A neighborhood in Tokyo that used to have only a few gay bars for older men. In recent years, however, there has been a succession of establishments opening in Shibuya aimed at the younger generation. It's gotten to the point that even a pamphlet called "Shibuya Gay Map" has been produced.

昨夜からずっと一緒だったね……

渋谷のゲイバーで飲みながら話す、大輔とマーク。
マークに改めて礼を言われ、大輔は少し、センチメンタルな気分に。

マーク：このお店も、ずいぶん混んでいますね。
大輔：うん。特に今日は、パレードの後だしね。
マーク：**渋谷★**には、何軒くらいゲイバーがあるんですか？
大輔：8軒くらいあるんじゃないかな。ここ数年で若い人向けのお店が、急に増えたみたいなんだ。
マーク：なるほど……。ところで大輔くん、昨夜も今日も、本当にありがとう。
大輔：どうしたの？ 急に改まって。
マーク：この二日間、とても楽しかったです。まさしさんにも良くしてもらったし、今日はパレード中に、大輔くんがいろいろと気を遣ってくれて……。嬉しかったです。
大輔：マーク、日本の夏は初めてだし、あんなに長い時間歩いて大丈夫かな、と思って。
マーク：明後日にはお別れだと思うと、さびしいですね。
大輔：うん。昨夜からほとんどずっと一緒にいたからね……。とにかく明日のレインボー祭りは、楽しもう！

渋谷……長い間渋谷には、年配の人向けのゲイバーが数軒あるだけだった。しかし数年前から、若い世代向けの店が次々にオープン。独自に「渋谷ゲイマップ」という冊子を作成するなど、盛り上がりを見せている。

Column 6

二丁目のさまざまなお店

Various kinds of establishments in Ni-chome

　二丁目にはレズビアン・ゲイ関係以外にも、さまざまなお店があります。北京風中華料理店「随園別館」やタイ料理店「バーン・キラオ」、韓国料理店「チング」をはじめ、飲食店はたくさんありますし、「VELVET OVERHIGH'M dmx」のように、ゲイバーでも観光バーでもない、「一般」のバーもあります。少し変わったところでは、社交ダンススタジオ「シノダ・スポーツダンスクラブ」や、おもちゃ屋「Yellow Submarine」、大きいサイズの服が充実している衣料品店「サカゼン」、二丁目のママ・マスター御用達の24時間営業スーパー「丸栄」などもあります。二丁目のバーやクラブに遊びに行く機会があったら、ついでに周辺を散歩してみてはいかがでしょう。「ゲイの街」として知られる二丁目の、また違った一面が見られるかもしれません。

Not only does Ni-chome contain lesbian and gay-related establishments, but all sorts of different kinds of businesses as well. There are a lot of eating and drinking establishments, including the Peking-style Chinese restaurant "Zuien Bekkan", the Thai restaurant "Baan Kirao," and the Korean restaurant "CHIN・GOO." There are also "ordinary" bars that are not gay bars or "kanko" (tourist) bars, such as "VELVET OVERHIGH'M dmx." Other slightly unusual businesses include the social dance studio, "Shinoda Sports Dance Club," as well as the toy store, "Yellow Submarine,"a clothes store for large-sized people, "Sakazen," and a 24-hour supermarket frequently patronized by "mamas" and "masters," "Maruei." Why don't you walk around and visit some of these shops while on your way to or back from gay bars or clubs in Ni-chome? You'll be sure to see another, different, face of Ni-chome, known generally as a gay town.

Scene 7
The only time Ni-chome has a festival each year!

年に一度の、祭りの夜

Dialog 1

That's what we call an "o-mikoshi."

Mark: Naka-dori seems to be the main venue for the Tokyo Rainbow Festival.

Miho: Although the sun is still shining, there's already a huge crowd.

Masashi: That's because this is the only time Ni-chome has a festival each year! Still, there'll be a lot more people once it gets darker. Don't say I didn't warn you!

Mark: Some people are carrying something over there.

Daisuke: That's what we call an **"o-mikoshi"** (portable shrine). Usually it houses a (portable) shrine, but this one seems to be carrying a "saka-daru" (wooden sake barrel), I think.

Mark: "Saka-daru"?

Daisuke: A wooden container for Japanese sake. These people seem to be lifting it so easily that I think it must be empty, however.

Mark: By the way, what kind of uniform are they wearing?

Daisuke: Those are called "happi." It's a traditional kind of dress that Japanese wear at festivals and the like, ever since ancient times. The headbands they are wearing are called "hachimaki," and the socks they have on their feet are called "tabi."

Mark: I see. Everything looks so sexy.

"o-mikoshi" A miniature, portable shrine carried by people in festivals in Japan, and believed to hold a Shinto god. Most "mikoshi" have a portable shrine aboard, but depending on the nature of the parent shrine, they may carry something else, such as a sacred tree, a doll, or even a phallic symbol.

あれは御神輿というんだよ

東京レインボー祭り当日。再び二丁目へやってきた4人。
祭りのオープニングを飾る神輿に興味を示すマーク。

マーク：仲通りが、「東京レインボー祭り」のメイン会場になるんですね。

美穂：まだ明るいのに、すごい人出ですね。

まさし：年に一度の、二丁目のお祭りだからね！ でもこれから夜がふけるにつれて、どんどん増えるわよ。覚悟しておいて！

マーク：何かかついだ人たちがやってきますね。

大輔：あれは、御神輿（おみこし）★というんだよ。普通は神殿なんかが乗っているんだけど、今、上に乗っているのは、酒樽かな？

マーク：酒樽？

大輔：日本酒を入れる、木で作られた容器だよ。あんなに軽々と担いでいるから、たぶん、中身は入ってないだろうけどね。

マーク：ところで彼らが着ているあの服は、何ですか？

大輔：法被（はっぴ）だよ。昔から日本人がお祭りの時なんかによく着る、伝統的な衣装なんだ。頭に巻いているのは鉢巻（はちまき）、足に履いているのは足袋（たび）だよ。

マーク：なるほど。とてもセクシーな格好ですね。

御神輿……日本の神社の祭りの際に人々が担ぐ、神霊を安置した輿（昔の乗り物）。小さな神殿が乗っているケースが多いが、その神社の性格によって、神木や人形、時には男根をかたどったものが乗っていることもある。

Dialog 2

There are sure a lot of food stalls here.

Miho: There are sure a lot of food stalls here. Some are selling beer, and others shaved ice.... There's even one selling chocolate-covered bananas!

Daisuke: The **Shinjuku Ni-chome Promotion Association** has cooperated in getting the stalls put up, I hear.

Masashi: Gay bars, club-type bars and "new half" show pub bars have gotten together to put the stalls up. It's interesting to see such normally unlikely combinations.

Daisuke: There was even a stall once, I heard, where you could throw water balloons at "mama-sans."

Masashi: That was quite thrilling. I wonder if it's up this year.

Mark: Oh, look! Over there! It's Raku from "ISLANDS." Reiko from "La SAISON" is here, too! ...Hello!

Reiko: why, if it isn't Mark!

Raku: So you've come to see the Rainbow Festival?

Mark: Yes. I'll have one beer, please.

Raku: Thank you! Have a great time at the Festival.

Mark: I will.

Shinjuku Ni-chome Promotion Association A union organization active since 2000, with a membership made up of various lesbian and gay eating and drinking establishments in Ni-chome. It sponsors the Tokyo Rainbow Festival and other events, and publishes the "Ni-chome Kawara-ban" newsletter. The current chairman is the owner of the gay bar, mf (mezzo-forte), Mitsuo Fukushima.

屋台もたくさん出ているのね

仲通りに出ているたくさんの屋台を眺めて歩く4人。
マークが、「アイランド」のラクと「ラ・セゾン」のレイコを発見する。

美穂：たくさん屋台が出てますね。ビールにかき氷に……。チョコバナナを売ってる屋台もある！

大輔：**新宿二丁目振興会**★に所属しているお店の人たちが、協力して屋台を出しているみたいだよ。

まさし：ゲイバーとクラブ系のバーとニューハーフショーパブが、一緒に一つの屋台をやっていたり……。普段なら考えられないような組み合わせがあって、面白いのよ。

大輔：バーのママに水風船をぶつける屋台もあるって聞いたことがあります。

まさし：あれはなかなかスリリングよ……。今年も出ているのかしら。

マーク：あ！　あそこに、「アイランド」のラクさんが。「ラ・セゾン」のレイコさんも！　……こんにちは。

レイコ：あら、マークじゃない！

ラク：レインボー祭り、観に来たんだ？

マーク：はい。ビール1本ください。

ラク：ありがとうございます！　お祭り、楽しんでいってくださいね。

マーク：はい。

新宿二丁目振興会……2000年から活動している、二丁目のレズビアン・ゲイ向けの飲食店が加盟している組合団体。東京レインボー祭りなどのイベントの開催、フリーペーパー「2丁目瓦版」の発行などを行っている。現会長は、ゲイバー「mf」のオーナー・福島光生。

Dialog 3

The Festival always closes with an "eisaa" dance.

Masashi: Oh, no! It's past 6:00 p.m. already. We ought to get close to the stage as early as we can.

Mark: You mean the place where that **band** was performing a short while back?

Masashi: Yeah. Later, there'll be a drag queen show and then an "eisaa" dance. We'll be unable to see them if we don't get there before it gets crowded.

Mark: What's an "eisaa?"

Daisuke: It's a "bon-odori" ("bon" dance) from Okinawa. The show time at the Rainbow Festival always closes with a performance by the LGBT Eisaa Team, and everyone does the dance together.

Masashi: Daisuke and everybody, shouldn't you make a bathroom stop before things start? I doubt if you'll be able to move around once you reach the stage. We'll be stuck there all the way from the show time until the DJ time and the release of the balloons at the ending.

Miho: Oh, my gosh! Let me go use the facilities then. Can you all wait for me here?

Masashi: Hurry!

---

band Since 2000, the number of LGBT artists and bands performing under the genre "gay indies" has been increasing, giving many live performances and putting out CDs.

お祭りの最後はエイサーで

祭りを堪能する4人。と、突然まさしが焦りだす。
急いでステージ近くへ戻らないと、パフォーマンスを見逃してしまうらしい。

まさし：いけない！　もう6時すぎちゃった。早くステージ近くに行かないと。

マーク：さっき、**バンド**★が演奏していたところですよね？

まさし：そう。この後、ドラァグクイーンのショーやエイサーが始まるんだけど、混む前に移動しないと、見逃しちゃう。

マーク：エイサーって何ですか？

大輔：沖縄の盆踊りだよ。レインボー祭りのショータイムの最後は必ず、LGBTのエイサーチームが演奏し、みんなでエイサーを踊ることになっているんだ。

まさし：大輔たち、トイレには行っておかなくて大丈夫？　一度ステージ前まで行ったら、ショータイムからDJタイム、エンディングの風船飛ばしまで、たぶん身動きがとれなくなっちゃうわよ。

美穂：大変！　私、ちょっと行ってくる。ここで待っててもらっていい？

まさし：急いで！

バンド……2000年頃から「ゲイ・インディーズ」と称して活動を行う、LGBTのアーティストやバンドが増えており、ライブ活動やCDのリリースなどを活発に行っている。

Dialog 4

Esmralda is going to do a show.

Daisuke: This year's Festival was a lot of fun, too!
Miho: The release of the balloons at the ending moved me so much. The colorful balloons floating in the night sky were so pretty!
Mark: A lot of people have stuck around after the end of the Festival.
Masashi: That's because many of them still have "o-bon" vacation tomorrow.
Ken'ichi: Masashi, hi!
Masashi: Oh, if it isn't Ken'ichi! What are you in a rush for?
Ken'ichi: Esmralda is going to do a show at a club event soon.
Daisuke: You mean Esmralda, the drag queen?
Ken'ichi: Yes.
Daisuke: I want to go, too. Mark and everyone else, won't you come along?
Mark: Sure. I've never been to a Japanese club event, either.
Miho: I'd like to go, too!
Masashi: It's been so long since I went to a club. I wonder if there are any cute **go-go** (boys) there.

---

go-go Short for "go-go boys," referring to guys hired to dance in provocative clothing or half-naked, so as to spice up events such as gay nights.

エスムラルダがショーをやるんですよ

祭りのあと、仲通りを歩く4人に、健一が声をかける。
ドラァグクイーンがクラブでショーをやると聞き、大輔たちも行ってみることに。

大輔：今年のお祭りも楽しかった……。
美穂：最後の風船飛ばし、感動しました。色とりどりの風船が夜空を飛んでいって、きれいだったなー。
マーク：お祭りが終わった後も、人がたくさん残っていますね。
まさし：明日もお盆休みの人が多いからね。
健一：まさしさん、こんばんは！
まさし：あら、健一じゃない。アンタ、何急いでんの？
健一：もうすぐ、エスムラルダがクラブイベントでショーをやるんですよ。
大輔：エスムラルダって、ドラァグクイーンの？
健一：そうです。
大輔：僕も観に行こうかな……。マークたちも、一緒にどう？
マーク：そうですね。まだ、日本のクラブイベントには一度も行ってないし。
美穂：私も行ってみたい！
まさし：クラブに行くなんて、久しぶりだわ……。かわいい**ゴーゴー**★の子とか、いるかしら。

ゴーゴー……「ゴーゴーボーイ」の略。ゲイナイトなどで、イベントを盛り上げるために、セクシーな衣装や半裸でダンスを踊る人のこと。

Dialog 5

They even hold a night for chubby chasers.

Masashi: There are several clubs in the Ni-chome vicinity that gays and lesbians like to go to, such as "club ArcH" and "BAR Hijoguchi."

Miho: There are a lot of flyers here.

Daisuke: Most of them are probably flyers for events that are going to take place here in the future.

Mark: I think I can get the drift of the events somehow, just by looking at the illustrations and photographs. This one is for a night for chubby chasers, right?

Daisuke: You got it! There's also a night for people wearing suits and those who have a fetish for such guys, as well as a night for college students, and another for those who like hip-hop. There's a whole lot of different events going on.

Miho: This is an event schedule ... there seems to be some kind of event practically every day.

Masashi: Around 20 years ago, there were only a few **gay nights** each month, at big clubs in Shibaura and Nishi-Azabu (in Tokyo). Each time one was held, we all got stirred up and saw some action. A lot of time has sure passed since then!

Daisuke: Masashi, you're getting that distant look again!

---

gay nights Regularly held throughout the year at several large clubs around Tokyo, and not just in Ni-chome. Especially well known is the giant club space "ageHa" in Shin-kiba, which can hold several thousand people, many of whom come from overseas. In recent years, there has been a surge in gay nights held in cities outside of Tokyo, too.

デブ専ナイトの日もあるんですね

二丁目のクラブ「club ArcH」へやって来た4人。
入り口にあるフライヤーのイラストを見て、イベントの内容を推測するマーク。

まさし：二丁目周辺には、ここ「club ArcH」や「BAR 非常口」など、いくつかのクラブがあって、レズビアンやゲイに親しまれているの。

美穂：フライヤーがたくさん置いてあるわね。

大輔：ほとんどが、今後、ここで行われるイベントのフライヤーなんじゃないかな。

マーク：イラストや写真を見ただけで、何となくイベントの趣旨がわかるような気がします。これは「デブ専ナイト」ですか？

大輔：当たり！ 他にも、スーツの人やスーツ好きな人が集まるナイト、大学生が集まるナイト、ヒップホップ好きな人が集まるナイト……いろんなイベントがあるんだよ。

美穂：ここにイベントスケジュールがあるけど……。ほぼ毎日、何かしらのイベントをやっているのね。

まさし：20年くらい前は、**ゲイナイト**★って、芝浦や西麻布の大きなクラブで、月に数回行われるだけだったの。その度にアタシたち、気合を入れて参戦したものよー。あれからたくさんの月日が流れたのね……。

大輔：まさしさん、また遠い目になってますよ……。

ゲイナイト……二丁目のクラブ以外にも、都内のいくつかの大きなクラブで、定期的にゲイナイトが開催されている。特に新木場の巨大クラブスペース「ageHa」のゲイナイトは、数千人の集客を誇り、海外からの客も多い。また近年、地方のゲイナイトが急増している。

Dialog 6

Japanese drag queens are really something else!

Daisuke : Esmralda's show is just beginning now!
Mark : What's that song?
Daisuke : It's called an "enka," a special kind of Japanese ballad, you could say. Esmralda's a **drag queen** who puts on a passionate show, performing in line with the words of the "enka."
Miho : My God! She's spitting up blood! How scary!
Mark : I've seen a whole lot of different performances, for these three days, but Japanese drag queens are really something else!
Masashi : Really? But New York is supposed to be the home of the true drag queen, isn't it?
Mark : That may be true, but I think Japanese drag queens have a leg up when it comes to originality. This is the first time I've seen a show with lines taken from a movie. In New York, the only kind of show I've seen is where the drag queen just lip-synchs. Although I couldn't understand what they were saying, it was a great new experience.
Masashi : That's because Japanese drag queens, overall, tend toward comedy. Of course there are also those who pursue ture beauty, too.

---

drag queen Someone who puts on flamboyant makeup and women's clothing to spice up club events and put on shows. Basically, drag queens put on an excessive parody of their female-ness, and are thus different from cross-dressers who just want to look like ordinary women.

日本のドラァグクイーンは面白いですね

フロアへ入るやいなや、ショーが始まる。
日本のドラァグクイーンについて語る、マークとまさし。

大輔：ちょうどエスムラルダのショータイムが始まった！

マーク：この曲は何ですか？

大輔：演歌だよ。日本独特の歌謡曲、といったらいいのかな。エスムラルダは、演歌に合わせて、情念系のショーをやる**ドラァグクイーン**★なんだ。

美咲：きゃ！　口から血を吐いた！　恐い！

マーク：この3日間、いろいろなパフォーマンスを観てきましたが、日本のドラァグクイーンは面白いですね。

まさし：本当？　ニューヨークなんてまさに、ドラァグクイーンの本場でしょ？

マーク：そうなんですが、日本のドラァグクイーンにはオリジナリティがある気がします。たとえば、映画のセリフを切り貼りしたショーをやっている人もいましたよね。ニューヨークでは、リップシンクのショーしか観たことがないので、言葉はわからなかったけど新鮮でした。

まさし：日本のドラァグクイーンは、全体的にお笑い方向に寄り気味だからね……。もちろん中にはちゃんと、キレイさを追求しているクイーンもいるけど。

ドラァグクイーン……派手なメイクや衣装に身を包み、クラブイベントなどを盛り上げたり、ショーをしたりする人。基本的には「女性性を過度にパロディ化したもの」であり、「普通の女性のようになることを目的とした女装」とは異なる。

Dialog 7

Are there particular artists popular among gays in Japan?

Masashi : They're playing quite a few oldies today.

Mark : Are there particular **artists popular among gays** in Japan, too? Just like Madonna (1958-) or Kylie Minogue (1968-).

Masashi : Gays of my generation in Japan pretty much like those two singers, too. I wonder if there are fans of artists like Madonna or Kylie Minogue in Daisuke's generation as well?

Daisuke : Hmm, there are some who are, but not so many, I think. I only listen to J-POP anyway.

Mark : J-POP?

Masashi : It's short for "Japanese pops." People in my generation like such singers as Yumi Matsutoya (1954-), Miyuki Nakajima (1952-), Seiko Matsuda (1962-), Dreams Come True (fronted by Miwa Yoshida, 1965-), and Noriyuki Makihara (1963-).

Daisuke : Nowadays it would be more like singers like Namie Amuro (1977-) and Ayumi Hamasaki (1978-). Amuro even came to this event once, incognito.

Miho : She did? Cool!

Masashi : There are a quite a lot of celebrities who owe their popularity to gays, as well as quite a few who like to come to Ni-chome just to have fun.

---

artists popular among gays   Gays tend to like female singers and male singers who sing in a feminine style. Gays also have a tendency of continuing to support singers whose popularity has faded among the general audience.

ゲイに人気の芸能人たち

引き続き「club ArcH」にて。DJの選曲を聴きながら、
「日本のゲイが好きなアーティスト」について語り合う4人。

まさし：今日はちょっと、懐かしめの曲が多いわね。
マーク：日本でも、マドンナやカイリー・ミノーグは、**ゲイに人気**★があるんですか？
まさし：アタシたちの世代は割とみんな好きだけど……。大輔たちの世代にも、マドンナとかカイリーのファンはいるのかしら。
大輔：うーん、好きな人は好きだと思うけど、そんなには多くないんじゃないかな。僕は、J-POPしか聴かないし。
マーク：J-POP？
まさし：日本のポップスのことよ。アタシたちの世代だと、松任谷由実や中島みゆき、松田聖子、ドリームズ・カム・トゥルー、槇原敬之なんかが人気よね。
大輔：今だと、安室奈美恵とか浜崎あゆみあたりかな。安室奈美恵は、ここで行われたイベントに、おしのびで来たこともあるんだよ。
美穂：そんなことがあったの？　すごい！
まさし：ゲイ人気に支えられている芸能人も、二丁目で遊ぶのが好きな芸能人も、結構多いのよね。

ゲイが好きなアーティスト……ゲイに人気があるのは、女性歌手や、女性的な歌を歌う男性歌手であることが多い。またゲイには、世間一般の人気が衰えた歌手などを応援し続ける傾向が強いとも言われている。

Dialog 8

I have something important to say to Mark now.

Masashi: Oh, that troublesome kid again....

Taro: We meet again, Sister Masako. And Mark, too! I feel fate is at work here.

Masashi: Keep your feelings to yourself! And the way you call him Mark, aren't you being overly familiar?

Taro: Mark, won't you come and dance with me over there?

Mark: Hmm, what should I do?

Daisuke: You're Taro, right? Sorry, but I have something important to say to Mark now.

Taro: What the...!? I guess it can't be helped. Well, see you later, Mark.

Masashi: It's a relief to know that jerk is gone. Be that as it may, it's quite unusual to see you, Daisuke, giving somebody the brush-off.

Daisuke: No, I really do have something to say to Mark.

Masashi: Good grief, I get the feeling that even I am in the way! Anyway, my favorite kind of **"o-ne-ha"** (**music**) is playing right now, so Miho, let's go over there and dance.

Miho: OK!

"o-ne-ha" (**music**) Short for house music that "o-né" (queenie gays) love. In particular, it refers to songs sung by diva-type female vocalists.

僕、今からマークに大事な話があるんだ

再び太郎に見つかってしまう4人。マークにアプローチをかける太郎を、
今回は大輔が退ける。そして、「マークに話がある」と言う大輔。

まさし：あら、また面倒くさい子がいるわ……。
太郎：まさ子ネエさん、また会いましたね。それにマークも！　何か運命感じちゃうなー。
まさし：勝手に感じてんじゃないわよ。しかもマーク、マークって、なれなれしいわね。
太郎：マーク、向こうで一緒に踊らない？
マーク：えーっと、どうしよう…。
大輔：太郎くんだっけ、ごめん。僕、今から、マークに大事な話があるんだ。
太郎：ええ!?　仕方ないなあ。じゃあマーク、後でね。
まさし：やれやれ、厄介なのがいなくなってホッとした。それにしても大輔、アンタが誰かを追い払うなんて珍しいわね。
大輔：いえ、実は本当にマークに話があるんです。
まさし：やだ、何だかアタシたちまで、お邪魔っぽい雰囲気ね……。ちょうどアタシ好みの**おネハ★**がかかってるし、美穂ちゃん、あっちで踊ってましょ。
美穂：はい！

おネハ……「おネエハウス」の略。ハウス・ミュージックのうち、おネエが大好きだとされている、「ディーバ系の女性ボーカルが歌い上げる」ような曲のことを指す。

Dialog 9

I'd be happy to be your "aikata."

Mark: Daisuke, what is it you wanted to talk about?

Daisuke: Well, you see.... You ended up not being able to find Yohei, right?

Mark: Yeah. Though I did look for him in the parade and at the Rainbow Festival site.

Daisuke: In such crowds, it would be impossible to find him anyway, even if he were there.

Mark: Well, it doesn't matter anymore anyway. There's someone else I've come to like.

Daisuke: What?! Who would that be? Someone I know?

Mark: You could say you know him.... It's you, Daisuke.

Daisuke: ...As a matter of fact, I was thinking during these past two days I spent with you, Mark, that I'd be happy to be your **"aikata" (partner)**.

Mark: ....

Masashi: Hey, you two! How come you're kissing?! When did you become a couple? Hey, Miho, something terrible has happened!

Daisuke: Masashi.... Give us a break! What great timing you have, interrupting us at a moment like this!

"aikata" (partner)   Originally a word referring to a partner in a "manzai" (stand-up comedy) duo, it has for some reason come to be used by an increasing number of gays in recent years to mean "lover" or "boyfriend."

相方になってもらえたら嬉しい

フロアの片隅で二人きりで話す、大輔とマーク。
実はお互いに、惹かれあっていることがわかり……。

マーク：大輔くん、話って何ですか？
大輔：そのう……。結局、ヨウヘイくんは見つからなかったんだよね？
マーク：はい……。パレードやレインボー祭りの会場でも、探してはみたんですが。
大輔：あんな人ごみの中じゃ、たとえいても、見つからないよね。
マーク：でも、もういいんです。僕には他に、好きな人ができたから。
大輔：ええ!?　それは、誰？　僕の知ってる人？
マーク：知っている人というか……。大輔くんです。
大輔：……。実は僕も、2日間マークと一緒にいる間に、その……。**相方**★になってもらえたら嬉しいな、と……。
マーク：……。
まさし：アンタたち！　何キスなんかしてんのよ！　いつの間にそんな関係に？　ちょっと美穂、大変よ！
大輔：まさしさん……。普通、このタイミングで邪魔するかなあ。ありえない……。

相方……もともとは「漫才コンビのパートナー」を指す言葉だが、近年何故か、「恋人」「彼氏」を意味する言葉として、「相方」を使用するゲイが増えている。

Dialog 10

Let's let the young couple be by themselves.

Miho: Hey, it's already gotten bright outside!

Masashi: Oh, I hate it! It's been a while since I pulled an all-nighter. It's bad for the skin. Daisuke, it's your fault for wanting to go to a club!

Daisuke: Here, here, going to a club once in a while won't hurt you!

Masashi: And so, what are you two going to do now? Mark, you head back to New York tomorrow, right?

Mark: Yeah....

Masashi: So I guess that means you're going to carry out an ultra-long-distance love affair, separated by the Pacific Ocean and North American continent, right?

Daisuke: We're going to talk it over at the hotel now.

Masashi: Oh, cripes, they're going to leave us out of it! Why don't you just go to Massachusetts or whatever and get your **same-sex marriage** certificate, and be done with it!

Daisuke: Massachusetts?

Masashi: Well, Miho, we seem to be in the way here. Let's let the young couple be by themselves. ...I say that, but I can't let you two go off together so easily! Anyway, let's have something to eat now. How 'bout going to a soba noodle shop!

Daisuke: Lay it off, would you, Masashi!

---

same-sex marriage   Marriage between two people of the same sex. An increasing number of countries and regions worldwide are giving legal recognition to same-sex marriages, offering homosexual couples the same legal rights as married male-female couples. However, Japan is not yet one of them.

あとは若い二人に任せて……

クラブイベントが終わり、「ホテルで、今後のことを話し合う」
という大輔とマークを、あくまでも邪魔しようとするまさし。

美穂：外が、すっかり明るくなってる!
まさし：やだもう、久しぶりにオールしちゃった。お肌に悪いわ。大輔、アンタがクラブに行きたいなんて言うからよ!
大輔：まあまあ、たまにはいいじゃないですか。
まさし：で? これから二人はどうするのよ? マーク、明日にはニューヨークに帰っちゃうんでしょ?
マーク：はい……。
まさし：じゃあ、太平洋とアメリカ大陸を挟んだ、超遠距離恋愛するってわけ?
大輔：それは、これからホテルで、二人で考えます。
まさし：ちくしょう、ぬけぬけと! ふん、マサチューセッツにでも行って、とっとと**同性婚**★しちまえ!
大輔：マサチューセッツって……。
まさし：じゃあ美穂、アタシたちはお邪魔みたいだから、あとは若い二人に任せて……。って、そう簡単に二人きりにはさせないよ! とりあえず、みんなで飯よ飯。蕎麦屋にでも行くわよ!
大輔：ちょっとまさしさん、勘弁してくださいよ……。

同性婚……同性同士の結婚のこと。世界には、同性結婚を法的に認めたり、男女の夫婦に準じる権利を、同性のカップルにも法的に認める国や地域が増えつつあるが、日本ではまだ認められていない。

Epilogue

You two really are in love.

Masashi: Hey, Daisuke and Miho. It's been a while!

Daisuke: Oh, Masashi. Sorry for being out of touch for so long.

Miho: Thanks for everything you did the other day! Mark is really grateful to you, Masashi.

Masashi: Yeah, I always find myself in the position of being thanked!

Daisuke: Hey, Masashi, don't be so down in the dumps.

Masashi: Don't you be the one to tell me that! So how's your long-distance relationship with Mark working out? It's been three months already. Is everything OK?

Daisuke: Yeah, so far.... After that time, we both bought Webcams, and now chat everyday online, face-to-face. With Skype, you can talk for free as long as you want.

Miho: Really? You're doing that? Cool!

Masashi: Things have gotten quite convenient nowadays....

Daisuke: Also, once my work quiets down, I think I'll take a long break and go to New York.

Masashi: My goodness! You two really are in love. You make me so jealous, I hate you!

そして、二人は……

マークが帰国して3ヶ月が立ち、久しぶりに顔を合わせた3人。
大輔とマークの遠距離恋愛話を聞かされる、まさしと美穂。

まさし：ちょっと大輔、美穂、久しぶりじゃない。
大輔：ああ、まさしさん。ご無沙汰してしまってすみません。
美穂：その節は、本当にありがとうございました！ マーク、まさしさんにすごく感謝してました。
まさし：アタシはどうせ、いつも感謝されるだけの存在よ……。
大輔：またまさしさん、落ち込まないでくださいよ。
まさし：お前が言うな！ で、どうなのよ。マークとの遠距離恋愛は。あれから3ヶ月たったけど、上手くいってるの？
大輔：はい、今のところは……。あれからさっそく、お互いにウェブカメラを買って、毎日ネットでテレビ電話しています。スカイプだと、どんなに話しても無料なので。
美穂：へー！ そんなことしてるんだ！ すごい！
まさし：ほんと、便利な時代になったわよね……。
大輔：あと、今抱えてる仕事がひと段落したら、長期休暇をとって、ニューヨークに行ってみようかと思って。
まさし：あらまあ！ 熱々ね。うらやましすぎて、ちょっと憎いわ……。

Index

あ

ILGA日本 ILGA Japan……19
相方 "aikata" (partner) ……175
赤線地帯 red-light district……15
アキバ系 "Akiba-kei"……83
akta ……63, 87, 93, 95, 97
『anise』 "anise"……103
安室奈美恵 Namie Amuro……171

い

イカニモ系 "ikanimo-kei" (someone obviously gay) ……35
イケメン "ikemen" (good-looking guy) ……129
居酒屋 Japanese "izakaya" pubs ……37, 39, 41, 55, 65, 115

う

ウーロン茶割り chuhai with Oolong……53, 55
ウケ "neko" (bottom)……61
歌声喫茶 choral café……57
売り専 "uri-sen" (money-boy) ……125, 127

え

エイサー eisaa……163
エイズ予防財団 Japanese Foundation for AIDS Prevention……95, 97
SNS (ソーシャル・ネットワーキング・サービス) SNS (social networking service) ……17, 134
SG系 SG types……83, 103, 105
エスムラルダ Esmralda……165, 169
『egg』 "egg"……128
HIV/AIDS ……59, 95, 97, 141
HIV感染者 HIV-positive people ……97
LGBT (レズビアン・ゲイ・バイセクシュアル・トランスジェンダー) LGBT (lesbian, gay, bisexual, transgender, and other sexual minorities) ……19, 107, 137, 143, 145, 147, 151, 153, 163
LGBTの政治家 LGBT politicians ……151
エルヴィン・ジョーンズ Elvin Jones ……67
演歌 "enka"……169

お

狼専 "okami" (wolf) fetish……87
オープンカフェ open-air café / bar ……79
オカマ fag……41, 137, 143
おしぼり "oshibori" towel……51
尾辻かな子 Kanako Otsuji……151
お通し "o-toshi" (small side

dishes)……55, 71
お仲間 "o-nakama" (one of us)……35
おなべバー "onabe" bar……119, 121
おネエ言葉 "o-né" (queenie) language……29
おネエ・MANS "O-né, MANS!"……107
おネハ "o-ne-ha" (music) ……173
お盆 "o-bon"……33, 165
御神輿 "o-mikoshi" (portable shrine)……159

か

『Carmilla』 "Carmilla"……103
会員制 Members only……49
外専 "gai-sen" (someone with a fetish for foreigners, especially Westerners)……23, 77, 81
カイリー・ミノーグ Kylie Minogue……171
楽器経験者 people who can play musical instruments……145
ガテン系 "gaten-kei"……83
がちぽちゃ "gachipocha"……83, 85
上川あや Aya Kamikawa……151
カミングアウト come out……31, 90, 103, 151
カラオケ karaoke……43, 57

観光バー "kanko" (tourist) bar……121, 156
関西レインボーパレード Kansai Rainbow Parade……147

き

キャッシュオンデリバリー cash on delivery……53

く

『Queer Japan Returns』 "Queer Japan Returns"……103
QUEEN ……90
熊系 "kuma-kei" (bear type)……83
熊専 "kuma-sen" (bear fetish)……87
組合の人 "kumiai no hito" (member of the union)……35
グリニッチヴィレッジ Greenwich Village……57
『CREA』 "CREA"……112

け

系 "kei" (type)……83
ゲイ・インディーズ gay indies……163
ゲイショップ gay shop……101
ゲイナイト gay nights……153, 165, 167

Index

ゲイ・ルネッサンス'91 Gay Renaissance '91……112
源氏名 "genji-na" (gay alias)……63

こ

倖田來未 Kumi Koda……90
紅白歌合戦 "Kohaku Uta-gassen" (Red-White Song Match)……109
ゴーゴー go-go……165
こっちの人 "kottchi no hito" (someone on this side)……35

さ

佐木隆三 Ryuzo Saki……46
札幌のパレード Sapporo Parade……147
『サムソン』 "SAMSON"……103

し

『シーメール白書』 "She-male"……103
『G-men』 "G-men"……102, 103
J-POP……170, 171
下着 underwear……101, 105
渋谷 Shibuya……17, 19, 153, 155
渋谷ゲイマップ Shibuya Gay Map……155
指名 point him out……127, 129
ジャニ系 "Johnny-style guys" (young, cute pop-idol type boys)……133
宿場 post station……15
出展ブース booths……141
趣味女 "shumi-jo" (hobby women)……45
成覚寺 Jokaku-ji……68
正受院 Shoju-in……68
ショットバー shot bar……71, 93
新宿ゴールデン街 "Shinkuku Golden-Gai" (Golden quarter)……46
新宿末廣亭 Shinjuku Suehiro-tei……37
新宿二丁目振興会 Shinjuku Ni-chome Promotion Association……19, 139, 161
新宿ピットイン Shinjuku Pit Inn……67
新宿遊郭 "Shinjuku Yukaku"……15
新千鳥街 Shin-Chidori-gai……89

す

スカイプ Skype……179
スーツ専 suits fetish……87
ステージイベント stage event……143

せ
セーファーセックス Safer sex……99
セーフセックス safe sex……97, 99
世田谷区議会議員選挙 Setagaya Ward Council elections ……151

そ
蕎麦屋 soba noodle shops……115, 177

た
太宗寺 Taiso-ji……68
タイニイアリス Tiny Alice……67
駄菓子 molded candies……105
タチ "tachi" (top) ……61
足袋 tabi……159
誰専 "dare-sen" (anybody OK) fetish……87

ち
チャンスボトル chance bottle……53

て
出会い系サイト dating websites ……17, 134
デブ専 "debu-sen" (chubby fetish) ……85, 103, 125, 167
デリヘルボーイ deli-hel boy……23, 59

と
東京プライドパレード Tokyo Pride Parade……19, 135, 137, 139
東京レインボー祭り Tokyo Rainbow Festival……19, 33, 159, 161
東郷健 Ken Togo……151
同性婚 same-sex marriage……177
ドラァグクイーン drag queens…… 137, 165, 167, 169
トランスヴェスタイト transvestites ……119
トランスジェンダー transgendered people……19, 119
ドリームズ・カム・トゥルー Dreams Come True……171
どんだけー！ "Don dake――!" ……107

な
内藤新宿 Naito Shinjuku……15
中上健次 Kenji Nakagami……46
中島みゆき Miyuki Nakajima ……171
仲通り Naka-dori……15, 67, 83, 101, 109, 115, 159, 161, 165
中野 Nakano……27

に
24会館 24 Kaikan……133
肉じゃが "niku-jaga"……41

Index

2丁目瓦版 "Ni-chome Kawara-ban" ……161
日本酒 Japanese sake……41, 159
ニューハーフ new half……23, 119, 121
ニューハーフショーパブ new half show pub bar……23, 119, 121, 123

ね

ネエさん "né-san" (sister) ……79, 81, 143, 173

の

ノンケ "nonke" (heterosexual) ……35, 45, 49, 90, 115, 121, 149

は

売春防止法 Anti-prostitution Act ……15
HUGS ……134
鉢巻 "hachimaki" ……159
ハッテン場 "hattenba" (cruising spot) ……17, 117, 131, 133
法被 "happi" ……159
『Badi』 "Badi" ……103
花園神社 Hanazono Shrine……46
浜崎あゆみ Ayumi Hamasaki ……139, 171
原宿駅 Harajuku Station……137
バンド band……163

ひ

B系 B-kei……83
BYGSビル BYGS Building……65
一重専 single-edged eyelid fetish ……87
日野皓正 Terumasa Hino……67
『ひまわり』 "Himawari" ……103

ふ

福島光生 Mitsuo Fukushima ……161
老専 "fuke-sen" bars (for guys with a preference for older guys) ……
藤圭子 Keiko Fuji……46
伏見憲明 Noriaki Fushimi……103
腐女子 "fujoshi" (rotten girls) ……109
ブス "busu" (ugly) ……123
ブス専 "busu-sen" (ugly fetish) ……87
ブラッド・ピット Brad Pitt……21
フレディ・マーキュリー Freddie Mercury……83, 90
フロート floats……19, 139, 149
ふんどしバー fundoshi bar……131

ほ

ホストクラブ host club……125
ボランティア volunteers……153

ま

槇原敬之 Noriyuki Makihara……171

マスター master……43, 53, 55, 83, 156

松田聖子 Seiko Matsuda……139, 171

松任谷由実 Yumi Matsutoya……171

マドンナ Madonna……171

ママ専 "mama-sen" (mama fetish)……87

み

mixi ……17, 134

南定四郎 Teishiro Minami……19

美輪明宏 Akihiro Miwa……90

"みんな"でブラス！ Brass with Everybody!……145

め

飯盛女 "meshimori-onna"……15

メンオンリー men only……75

Men's mixjp ……134

も

桃組 Pink Team……109

や

屋台 food stalls……115, 141, 161

山下洋輔 Yosuke Yamashita……67

ゆ

百合の小道 Lily Path……93

よ

代々木公園 Yoyogi Park……137, 139, 147

ら

ライスクイーン "rice queen" (you have to suffer) ……77

り

リップシンク lip-synching……149, 169

る

ルミ子 Lumiko……101

れ

rainbow arts……111

RAINBOW RING……69, 95

レインボーフラッグ rainbow flag ……49, 149

レズビアンバー lesbian bars……93

わ

若専 "waka-sen" (you prefer young guys) ……73

渡辺貞夫 Sadao Watanabe……67

Information

advocates café tokyo
1F 7th Tenka Bldg.,2-18-1,
Shinjuku,Shinjuku-ku,Tokyo
03-3358-3988
【open】18:00-4:00, 18:00-1:00 (Sun. and holidays)
Open Every Day

akta
#301 2nd Nakae Bldg.,2-15-13,
Shinjuku,Shinjuku-ku,Tokyo
03-3226-8998
【open】16:00-22:00
【closed】2nd Sun.

ANDERSEN
2-18-10,Shinjuku,Shinjuku-ku,Tokyo
03-3341-0392
【open】16:00-2:00
Open Every Day

ARTY FARTY HEADQUARTER
2F 33rd Kyutei Bldg.,2-11-7,
Shinjuku,Shinjuku-ku,Tokyo
03-5362-9720
【open】19:00-3:00,19:00-5:00 (Fri.&Sat.),
　　　 17:00-3:00 (Sun. and holidays)
Open Every Day

BALZAAL
1F Osu Bldg.,2-15-12,Shinjuku,Shinjuku-ku,Tokyo
03-3341-6505
【open】15:00-0:00, 15:00-2:00 (Fri.&Sat.)
Open Every Day

BAR HIJOGUCHI
1F Sentfour Bldg.,2-12-16,
Shinjuku,Shinjuku-ku,Tokyo
03-3341-5445
【open】19:00-5:00
【closed】Sun.

advocates café tokyo
東京都新宿区新宿2-18-1　第7天香ビル1F
03-3358-3988
【営】18:00-4:00, 18:00-1:00 (日・祝)
無休

コミュニティセンター・アクタ
東京都新宿区新宿2-15-13
第2中江ビル301
03-3226-8998
【開】16:00-22:00
【休】第2日曜

アンデルセン
東京都新宿区新宿2-18-10
03-3341-0392
【営】16:00-2:00
無休

ARTY FARTY HEADQUARTER
東京都新宿区新宿2-11-7　第33宮廷ビル2F
03-5362-9720
【営】19:00-3:00, 19:00-5:00 (金・土),
　　　17:00-3:00 (日・祝)
無休

通販バディ&メンズオリジナルショップ・バルザール
東京都新宿区新宿2-15-12　大須ビル1F
03-3341-6505
【営】15:00-0:00, 15:00-2:00 (金・土)
無休

BAR　非常口
東京都新宿区新宿2-12-16 セントフォービル1F
03-3341-5445
【営】19:00-5:00
【休】日

club ArcH
B1F 2nd Hayakawaya Bldg.,2-14-6,
Shinjuku,Shinjuku-ku,Tokyo
03-3352-6297
【open】19:00-5:00,
　　　17:00-5:00（Fri.&Sat. and holidays)
Open Every Day

CoCoLo cafe
1F 1st Hayakawaya Bldg.,2-14-6,
Shinjuku,Shinjuku-ku,Tokyo
03-5366-9899
【open】17:00-5:00,17:00-7:00（Fri.),15:00-7:00（Sat.),
　　　15:00-4:00（Sun.and holidays)
【closed】1st Mon.

CONVOY
1F 3rd Tenka Bldg.,2-14-8,
Shinjuku,Shinjuku-ku,Tokyo
03-3341-1775
【open】12:00-4:00
Open Every Day

DraGon
1F Stork Nagasaki Bldg.,2-11-4,
Shinjuku,Shinjuku-ku, Tokyo
03-3341-0606
【open】18:00-4:00
Open Every Day

Fuji
B104 Sentfour Bldg.,2-12-16,
Shinjuku,Shinjuku-ku,Tokyo
03-3354-2707
【open】20:00-3:00,20:00-5:00（weekend)
Open Every Day

GB Tokyo
B1F Shinjuku Plaza Bldg.,2-12-3,
Shinjuku,Shinjuku-ku,Tokyo
03-3352-8972
【open】20:00-2:00,
　　　20:00-3:00（Fri.&Sat.and before holidays)
Open Every Day

club ArcH
東京都新宿区新宿2-14-6　第2早川屋ビルB1F
03-3352-6297
【営】19:00-5:00, 17:00-5:00（金・土・祝)
無休

ココロカフェ
東京都新宿区新宿2-14-6　第1早川屋ビル1F
03-5366-9899
【営】17:00-5:00,17:00-7:00（金），
　　　15:00-7:00（土），15:00-4:00（日・祝)
【休】第1月曜

コンボイ新宿店
東京都新宿区新宿2-14-8　第3天香ビル1F
03-3341-1775
【営】12:00-4:00
無休

DraGon
東京都新宿区新宿2-11-4　ストークビル長崎1F
03-3341-0606
【営】18:00-4:00
無休

Fuji
東京都新宿区新宿2-12-16　セントフォービルB104
03-3354-2707
【営】20:00-3:00,20:00-5:00（週末)
無休

GB Tokyo
東京都新宿区新宿2-12-3　新宿プラザビルB1F
03-3352-8972
【営】20:00-2:00,20:00-3:00（金・土・祝前)
無休

Information

ISLANDS
3F Imai Bldg.,3-11-1,Shinjuku,Shinjuku-ku,Tokyo
03-3359-0540
【open】19:00-2:00,
　　　　19:00-4:30 (Fri.&Sat. and before holidays)
【closed】Tue.

Kusuo
3F Sunflower Bldg.,2-17-1,
Shinjuku,Shinjuku-ku,Tokyo
03-3354-5050
【open】20:00-4:00
Open Every Day

La SAISON
3F Polestar Bldg.,2-19-9,
Shinjuku,Shinjuku-ku,Tokyo
03-3359-8861
【open】20:00-3:30
【closed】Sun.&3rd Mon.

LUMIERE
1F Sunflower Bldg.,2-17-1,
Shinjuku,Shinjuku-ku,Tokyo
03-3352-3378
【open】11:00-7:00
Open Every Day

THE ANNEX
1F Futami Bldg. ,2-14-11,
Shinjuku,Shinjuku-ku,Tokyo
03-3356-5029
【open】19:00-3:00,19:00-5:00 (Fri.&Sat),
　　　　17:00-3:00 (Sun. and holidays)
Open Every Day

24 Kaikan
2-13-1,Shinjuku,Shinjuku-ku,Tokyo
03-3354-2424
【open】24hours a day
Open Every Day

アイランド
東京都新宿区新宿3-11-1　今井ビル3F
03-3359-0540
【営】19:00-2:00,19:00-4:30（金・土・祝前）
【休】火

九州男
東京都新宿区新宿2-17-1　サンフラワービル3F
03-3354-5050
【営】20:00-4:00
無休

ラ・セゾン
東京都新宿区新宿2-19-9　ポールスタービル3F
03-3359-8861
【営】20:00-3:30
【休】日,第3月曜

ルミエール
東京都新宿区新宿2-17-1　サンフラワービル1F
03-3352-3378
【営】11:00-7:00
無休

THE ANNEX
東京都新宿区新宿2-14-11　フタミビル1F
03-3356-5029
【営】19:00-3:00, 19:00-5:00（金・土）,
　　　17:00-3:00（日・祝）
無休

24会館
東京都新宿区新宿2-13-1
03-3354-2424
【営】24時間
無休

※2008年4月のデータです。お店に行く場合はご確認ください。

●著者
森村明生
もりむら・あきお

1972年生まれ。一橋大学社会学部卒業。ライター兼ホラー系ドラァグクイーン（エスムラルダ。東京都ヘブンアーティスト）。携帯サイト「公募懸賞ガイド」、雑誌「CDジャーナル」「フォアミセス」等に、コラムや漫画原作を執筆中。

●訳者
Paul Narum
ポール・ネルム

アメリカ人。1959年生まれ。日本で幅広い分野で翻訳活動（和英）に従事する他に、大学講師や雑誌編集にも携わっている。初来日は少年時代の65年だが、定住してから30年近くなる。80年代半ばは東京大学で国際関係論の修士号を修得。海外旅行は100カ国・地域におよぶ。現在神奈川県在住。

●監修者
松沢呉一
まつざわ・くれいち

1958年生まれ。ライター。「実話ナックルズ」「スナイパーEVE」「お尻倶楽部」などで連載するかたわら、有料メルマガ「マッツ・ザ・ワールド」を毎月、原稿用紙換算で700枚から1000枚以上配信。著書に『熟女の旅』（ちくま文庫）、編著に『売る売らないはワタシが決める』（ポット出版）などがある。

書名	英語で新宿二丁目を紹介する本
副書名	Guiding Your Friends Around Shinjuku Ni-chome in English
著者	森村明生
訳者	ポール・ネルム
監修	松沢呉一
編集	那須ゆかり・沢辺均
英文編集協力	北丸雄二
ブックデザイン	山田信也
企画原案	高島利行（株式会社語研）
発行	2008年5月23日 ［第一版第一刷］
定価	1,600円＋税
発行所	ポット出版 ［株式会社スタジオ・ポット］

150-0001 東京都渋谷区神宮前2-33-18#303
電話　03-3478-1774
ファックス　03-3402-5558
ウェブサイト　http://www.pot.co.jp/
電子メールアドレス　books@pot.co.jp
郵便振替口座　00110-7-21168 ポット出版

印刷・製本 —— 株式会社シナノ

ISBN978-4-7808-0116-3　C0082
©2008 MORIMURA Akio, Paul Narum

Guiding Your Friends Around
Shinjuku Ni-chome in English
by:MORIMURA Akio, Paul Narum
First published in Tokyo Japan, May 23, 2008
by Pot Pub.Co.,ltd.
#303 2-33-18 Jingumae Shibuya-ku
Tokyo,150-0001 JAPAN
www.pot.co.jp
books@pot.co.jp
Postal transfer:00110-7-21168

ISBN978-4-7808-0116-3　C0082

書籍DB●刊行情報
1 データ区分 —— 1
2 ISBN —— 978-4-7808-0116-3
3 分類コード —— 0082
4 書名 —— 英語で新宿二丁目を紹介する本
5 書名ヨミ —— エイゴデシンジュクニチョウメヲショウカイスルホン
7 副書名 —— Guiding Your Friends Around Shinjuku Ni-chome in English
13 著者名1 —— 森村明生
14 種類1 —— 著
15 著者名1ヨミ —— モリムラアキオ
16 著者名2 —— ポール・ネルム
17 種類2 —— 訳
18 著者名2ヨミ —— Narum, P(Paul)
19 著者名3 —— 松沢呉一
20 種類3 —— 監修
21 著者名3ヨミ —— マツザワクレイチ
22 出版年月 —— 200805
23 書店発売日 —— 20080523
24 判型 —— B6判
25 頁数 —— 192
27 本体価格 —— 1600
33 出版社 —— ポット出版
39 取引コード —— 3795

本文●ホワイトアスワン・四六判・Y目・68kg(0.130) ／スミ
見返し●タント D70・四六判・Y目・100kg
表紙●アラベール・スノーホワイト・四六判・Y目・200kg ／TOYO 10441
カバー・オビ●リ・シマメ・クリームホワイト・四六判・Y目・100kg ／マットスミ＋TOYO 10441 ／マットPP
使用書体●游明朝体M＋PGaramond　ゴシックMB　中ゴシック　太ゴ　見出しゴ　PFrutiger　Frutiger
2008-0101-4.0

語研とポット出版による出版社を超えたコラボレーション第一弾

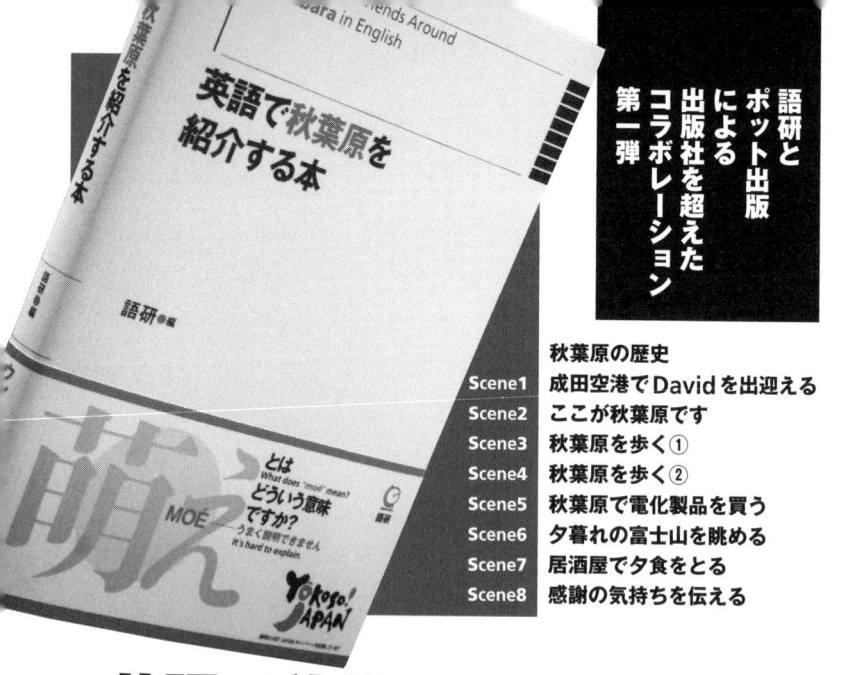

	秋葉原の歴史
Scene1	成田空港でDavidを出迎える
Scene2	ここが秋葉原です
Scene3	秋葉原を歩く①
Scene4	秋葉原を歩く②
Scene5	秋葉原で電化製品を買う
Scene6	夕暮れの富士山を眺める
Scene7	居酒屋で夕食をとる
Scene8	感謝の気持ちを伝える

英語で秋葉原を紹介する本
Guiding Your Friends Around Akihabara in English

編●語研　発売●語研

今や世界中の観光客から注目される"AKIBA"をストーリー仕立ての和英対訳で紹介。
アメリカからやってきたちょっとオタクな親子を連れて
秋葉原を観光案内することになった日本の普通の親子。
ライトでポップな秋葉原を堪能した後は、
都庁の展望室で富士山を眺め、高円寺で寿司や焼き鳥に舌鼓を打ちます。
本文だけでなく、各ページで紹介するアキバ文化や日本の食などに関する解説やウンチク、
章末のコラムも全て日本語・英語併記。
日本語を読んでいくだけでもクールな日本の再発見ができる
楽しい読みものになっています。

2008.04発行／定価1,680円(税込)　／ISBN978-4-87615-172-1 C0082／B6判／192ページ／並製

●**全国の書店・オンライン書店で購入・注文いただけます。**
●**以下のサイトでも購入いただけます。**
版元ドットコム　http://www.hanmoto.com/

※こちらの書籍は出版社の壁を超えた共同企画として語研からの発売となります。
本書籍の購入に関するお問い合わせ等は語研営業部までお寄せ下さい。

株式会社語研　〒101-0064　東京都千代田区猿楽町2-7-17
TEL：03-3291-3986　FAX：03-3291-6749　URL http://www.goken-net.co.jp/